dixi
books

Julian Rose

Julian Rose was born in March 1947, on the Hardwick Estate in South Oxfordshire's Chiltern Hills, the youngest of four children to the heir of the thousand acre estate and baronetcy, passed down from his great grandfather.

On leaving school, Julian sought to harmonise strong artistic aspirations with the demands and responsibilities of his new found role as a 'landowner'.

Returning to the UK in 1967, he worked alongside his mother, developing the estate's farming and forestry enterprises. In 1969 he moved to London and won a place at the Royal Academy of Dramatic Art, going on to work in regional repertory theatres as an actor/stage manager.

He moved back to Hardwick in 1983, to become a full time farmer, completing the conversion of the estate to organic farming methods, a process started in 1975, making him one of the pioneers of this ecological land management system. Joining the board of the Soil Association in 1984, Julian became involved in an intense campaign to promote ecological food and farming in the face of the rapid rise of industrial agriculture.

Julian also gained notoriety as both a defender and promoter of holistic approaches to the rejuvenation of struggling rural economies. Notably his unremitting insistence on the need to support local and regional, as opposed to 'global', food economies. An approach coined in a formula he named "The Proximity Principle". He sought to raise awareness of the need to build a dynamic balance between economic, social and environmental concerns. Never just one or the other.

In 1990 he took on the position of agricultural correspondent of the green broadsheet 'Environment Now', becoming one of the first UK activists to warn of the impending dangers of genetically modified foods.

In 2000 Julian was invited to become a co-director of the International Coalition to Protect the Polish Countryside, co-launching a highly successful 'Campaign for a GMO Free Poland' as well as leading a high profile defense of peasant farmers whom he holdsup as the true guardians of biodiversity throughout the world.

Creative Solutions to a World in Crisis

The Power of Locality

Julian Rose

Dixi Books

"This book is the second edition of 'Changing Course for Life' which was previously published in February 2009".

Creative Solutions to a World in Crisis
Julian Rose
Editor: Luise Hemmer Pihl
Designer: Pablo Ulyanov
Printed in Bulgaria
II. Edition: September 2018

Library of Congress Cataloging-in Publication Data
Julian Rose, 1947.
Creative Solutions to a World in Crisis / Julian Rose – 2nd ed.
ISBN: 978-619-7458-21-3
1. Ecology 2. Adult Non-Fiction 3. Essay

© Dixi Books Publishing OOD
9, Pozitano Str. Entr. B, Fl 1, Office 2, 1000, Sofia, Bulgaria
Lebuser Strasse 14, 10243, Berlin, Germany
info@dixibooks.com

Creative Solutions to a World in Crisis

The Power of Locality

Julian Rose

dixi
books

The Voice of the New Age

This book is dedicated to all those who seek the truth and wish to use it to transform our planetary way of life.

Special thanks to Jadwiga Lopata for her ceaseless encouragement and thoughtful comments.

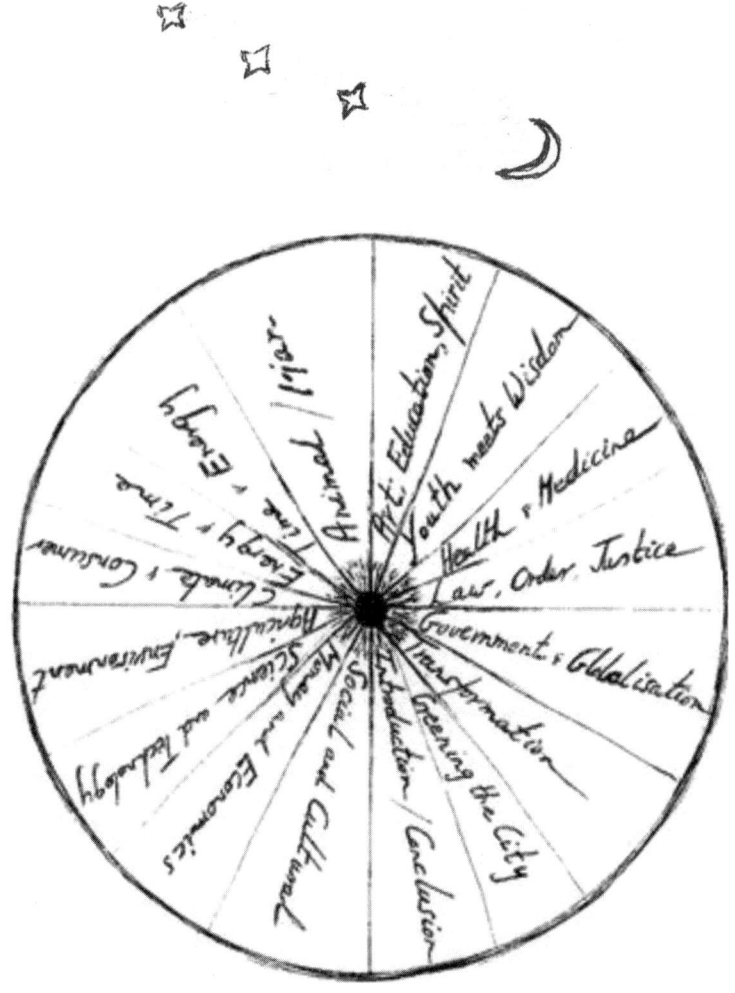

Contents

*P*reface for New Issue of Changing Course for Life

Friends,

I am very pleased that Dixi Books have decided to relaunch Changing Course for Life under its new title. The information it carries is even more relevant today, as global problems threaten to swamp local solutions. Solutions that contain all the right ingredients to greatly ameliorate the crisis that surrounds us at this apocalyptic moment in the history of the planet.

We humans are full of creative potential, but all too often find ourselves pouring this talent into daily work experiences that leave no scope for its expression. This is one of the first areas of 'wasted energy' that we need to face up to if we are to make a positive impact on our surroundings and fellow travellers.

After all, how long do each of us have on this beautiful planet? No one knows; but what they do know is that around 70% of the time we spend here, is devoted to trying to earn enough money to survive and prosper. Most of our energy lands up helping irresponsible corporations improve their profit margins, while we find ourselves becoming increasingly 'cyborgian', in debt and stuck firmly in the nine to five daily grind.

It is time to take a brave step away from the cruel hoax that ties us into this treadmill. It's time to leap into the beckoning world of creative commitment to change for the better. That which expresses our real reason for being here in the first place. There are a plethora of 'real jobs' to be done on our beleaguered planet, all of them calling out for a nurturing and compassionate approach to that which nourishes and provides for us, but which is forgotten in the rush to 'make it' in the commercial world of material ambition.

Between the covers of this small book you will find guidance concerning this path I'm encouraging you to take. You can jump in anywhere, as each chapter tells its own story and expresses its own passion for positive outcomes. However, if you start at the beginning and read on – you will discover a certain rhythm, a certain melodic theme, which develops as one goes along.

Life is an art, but not one to be practised in seclusion. The art of living is in joining together and facing, head-on, the often seemingly impossible challenges that confront us all. This is the way to banish fear and to bring joy into our lives and the lives of others. That is our calling – and nothing else should be allowed to deviate us from following that path.

Julian Rose
May 2018

*P*reface

"In a time of universal deceit telling the truth is a revolutionary act." George Orwell

Our present system of 'democracy' has failed us and it has failed our planet. Those who hold positions of power are neither able nor willing to face up to reality, let alone arrive at a common agreement how to deal with it. Because of this, we have to take over.

You are sitting on the couch watching television, the relentless and often apocalyptic news items, the compensatory superficial entertainment, the false smiles and pretty pictures – the whole commercial and politically driven package. For so long you have allowed yourself to slip under the beguiling influence of this package.

But suddenly you realise that it is a carefully constructed and strictly censored sham, and that you can't stand it anymore. You jump up from the sofa with a newly acquired sense of resolution – and turn off the set. It's a crucial step in the new journey you are about to embark on; the first step in changing course for life.

This book explores the background to these failings and the actions needed to reverse them, in order to achieve lasting, positive change. It is a truly exciting, challenging and necessary task. Since the rot is severely advanced in all spheres of society, only bottom-up, root and branch reform can effectively heal the sickness.

We have to take back control over our lives and reorder society from the foundations up. In so doing, we will reinvent communities, revive our own sense of purpose and light a cleansing fire that will eventually transform the way we live, sweeping clean the power mongers in the process.

This process has already begun, sporadically, and in pockets, but now we need the courage and conviction to engage in it on a broader scale and with a real sense of urgency.

The immediate aim is to transform local and regional government authorities into dynamic 'hubs' of people led resistance to negative change, and into active centres of positive change. Instead of taking piecemeal steps in one or two areas of outstanding concern, be they environmental, economic, cultural, medical etc. – we are called upon to set in motion the necessary steps that will eventually lead to a complete overhaul of *all* the component parts of our everyday way of life... because every one of them is suffering a crisis of similar magnitude, and only by tackling the totality can we achieve genuine change for the better.

In order to create genuine forward momentum on the ground we have to know what we mean and understand by 'education', 'culture', 'justice', 'energy', 'economics' and 'government'. We have to see how they connect up with each other and in what way they can be transformed and brought back to life; thus healing the deep wounds and schisms caused by decades of misinterpretation, neglect and abuse.

Many valuable environmental and community actions are already in existence all over the world. Every day new ones are starting up, and little beacons of light can be detected everywhere.

However, a quantum leap in applied creativity, imagination and practical skills is now needed to offset, and ultimately overcome, the unabating levels of destruction simultaneously manifesting themselves all around us. Destruction, not just of our environment and planetary resources, but of the values and ethics that keep societies healthy and secure. The callous disregard that most of our political figureheads show for anything other than their own morbid fascination in the power game, should, by now, have woken us up to the realisation that it is pointless, and even downright destructive, to keep re-electing them.

If we continue to play by the rules of this political game, we can expect to suffer at the hands of our own foolishness. We have to change the rules and the game, uniting our energies and channelling our creativity into actions whose roots are firmly planted in a process of local and regional rejuvenation. And, at the same time, we finally have to be able to say a resounding NO to the constant stream of debilitating and seductive compromises that so easily trap and enslave our unwary souls into submission to the moribund 'status quo'.

Continuously accepting ever more restrictive clamps upon our civil liberties and human aspirations ultimately weakens and confuses us, making us cannon fodder for the all consuming appetites of corporate pirates and political apologists.

There is nothing more important to do now than to take the authority to control our lives out of such people's hands, and to pour our energies into securing a resurgent future for largely self-governing human scale communities throughout the world.

Every day, small, well intentioned actions, directed towards this end can be taken by us all – bigger actions will soon follow. Then one day, as the momentum builds, great results will be manifest and a process of transformation will come about. We only need to get started – *and not give up.*

Julian Rose
January 2009

*I*ntroduction

"The world is a dangerous place, not because of those who do evil, but because of those who look on and do nothing."
Albert Einstein

It was at some point in my early thirties that I recall having the first thoughts of writing a book.

It was a quiet and somewhat distant voice at that time, but quite persistent. However, over two decades later, in 2007, on a pleasant late June evening in the Malopolska village of Stryszow (Poland), the event suddenly sprung to life. This time the call demanded immediate attention.

I was describing at some length the need to draw up a plan to comprehensively reform and reorder society from the bottom up. Some special gatherings would be needed, I suggested, bringing together key individuals able to help launch a comprehensive action plan.

When I finished my description, Jadwiga Lopata, my partner, (being of a direct Polish nature) simply said "It's a book, it is meant for many people to read and respond to."

As the sun slowly set over the Beskidi hills, I gradually absorbed this information. Somehow I knew it to be true. The sun set, and a silvery crescent moon rose in its place. It was a beautiful clear evening. At a forty-five degree angle from the centre of the crescent moon, rising up into the night sky were three bright stars, symmetrically spaced and crystal clear.

Now, dear reader, I want to share with you the outcome

of the seven intensive months which followed, in -and between- three countries: Poland, England and India, all places where we are actively pursuing an intensive campaign to highlight the values of traditional and ecological farming practices and to try and raise support to rid the world of genetically modified organisms.

Essentially, all the book revolves around -and relates to- the implementation of an action plan to "take control of life/our lives at the local level."

Each chapter is presented as a self contained essay. Each essay encompasses a different, yet closely connected expression of one overall concern: just as many refractions of light emanate from one diamond. Our ability to aid the great curing and healing process that our planet and ourselves must undergo, rests upon a deepening recognition that our living, breathing cosmos with its vast diversity of stars and planets, is manifest as a 'oneness of many parts'.

The many parts (of life) are dealt with by giving a chapter to each key earthly concern: i.e. Environment, Agriculture, Culture, Spirit, Economics, Science, Energy, Education, Communication, Art, Politics, Climate, Health and Justice. In each of these spheres, the book explores what has gone wrong, and proposes specific reforms required to transform our society for the better.

It is essentially a call to action, a manual for change. I would never have attempted to write such a book in any other spirit than this. It speaks to the Universal Spirit in all of us which longs for deep and lasting change – and is prepared to go out and fight for it.

February 2008

1. Social and Cultural
Back to the Beginning

Social and cultural expressions evolved around our need to come together in order to share common workloads and enjoy common pleasures. Crop planting and gathering, shelter construction and the wider establishment of human settlements; hamlets, villages, towns, all reflect our need -and desire- to live and work side by side. In the ritualised celebrations that marked the culmination of good work, we forged new links, bonds and cultural expressions that helped to bind and give social cohesion to our way of life. But these ties, forged over the millennia, are disappearing and no longer knitting communities together. Consequently, the fabric of our society is fraying at the seams, and no new binding force has yet emerged to pull it together again.

So, what has gone wrong?

At a time of (illusory) surplus of the necessities of life (in post-industrial societies) we have lost the will and sense of necessity that, in the past, drew us together in order to achieve our basic needs and physical nourishment. Since the advent of the industrial revolution, man has not only devised technological advances to free society from the ex-igencies of physical labour, but also from the need to share the work load with his neighbours. This has also removed one of the main incentives to come together in order to celebrate joyfully the completion of work; around the table, in the barns and on the fields.

Specialisation in the field of production of goods has separated tasks that were once co-mingled. In the home, TV and computers have drawn us away from shared games and simple social intercourse. The modern day 'entertainment industry' has succeeded in externalising fun and excitement, thereby removing it from the immediacy of family and the living social unit.

Even the microwave oven and the dish washer have joined the conspiracy, removing the need to share the tasks of food preparation, and the cleaning of food utensils. "Many hands make light work" is out of fashion; and hands themselves are now considered more important for tapping computer keyboards than for executing the manual skills associated with meeting our essential needs.

Man has therefore become steadily more estranged from his fellow men in direct proportion to the invention (and adoption) of labour saving technologies and with the steady increase in personal wealth. This process evolved out of a belief that technologies would free us to pursue more 'desirable' activities, or have more time for leisure. Social cohesion is thus the victim of a steadily growing quest for personal self-satisfaction, seen as something separate and abstracted, from the camaraderie of the immediate working environment.

The accumulation of wealth has been a crucial tool for reaching this goal. 'Making money' is, by and large, an antisocial process when it comes to healthy interactions with fellow human beings. It is antithetical to the true expression of our social needs. Indirectly, it has led to us being able to communicate with each other via computers and cell phone texts, so that even the intimacy of a voice on the telephone can be dispensed with. The seemingly magnetic attraction for speed, convenience and affordable consumables, has not been conducive to deeper human interaction and development, which has been left far behind in the rush to capitalise on largely superficial material satisfactions.

Such a protracted sense of separation between man and man is fuelled by increasingly intense, and often aggressive, competition in almost all walks of life. Success increasingly depends on a free market 'survival of the fittest' approach to life, leaving a string of casualties in its wake, and ultimately failing both man and nature.

Modern man has been educated to operate like a machine – programmed to make money – and in this way has ended up imitating the very machine that was supposed to liberate him. As our starved social instincts run perilously close to dry, our machines and gizmos assume ever greater importance, diverting us from confronting deeper and more pressing issues – including the realisation of solutions to the crisis facing our planetary existence.

Basic socio-cultural patterns of human behaviour develop out of the dynamics of community life. They have their roots in rural village communities where the daily movement of people between their places of work, their homes and their place of worship, build a patchwork pattern of simple connectivity, coupled to a certain basic rhythm of life. Fields were the main places of work for such communities, followed by blacksmiths, bakers, butchers, millers, cobblers and so on. Each local business increased the field of interactivity of village life, and one can freely sense how such a society grew into a form of extended family – everyone interacting with everyone else and sharing each others' common concerns.

It is hard to imagine any more organic way of devising a civilised community than through such simple social interaction. The architecture and design of the villages and market towns (that remain intact) seem to be 'calling us back', because they still resonate with our subconscious memories of a simple community life and the 'sense of belonging' that is, it turns out, impossible to dispense with.

As architecture, pictures, writings and memories remind us – like a mirror of the qualities we no longer maintain – present day unsustainable and crime ridden metropolises are not the best models for community living. We should be shocked into recognising that we cannot actually dispense with the simple qualities of what seems like a bygone era. The fact is, it is an era that lives on in our psyches, even if it has been largely wiped off our physical map.

Those fortunate enough to be able to afford to have been moving out of cities and into the rural villages and small towns of their ancestors. But in so doing, they have inflated the price of homes that once belonged to the artisans, farmers and shopkeepers, and inevitably, have also brought the vibrations of an urban lifestyle with them.

However, in spite of the confusion of conflicting attitudes and aspirations, this does not have to be a bad co-mingling; there are often positive outcomes to the blending of these different energies waiting in the wings. However, a common point of focus is vital – a goal shared by all – to ultimate success.

In an age of global market places, agribusiness and mass commuting, villages have inevitably suffered a steady death of community spirit, and the almost complete loss of necessity based lifestyles. Throughout much of Europe, most are today, pretty (or not so pretty) pictures of a secluded and sedentary way of life, that provides (at best) a certain enclave from the frenetic pace of the metropolis and encircling motorways.

To suggest that such places could once more burst into life as models of social and cultural entrepreneurial creativity, might seem absurd; yet that is just what this book is calling for, and is something I remain convinced is a genuinely realisable goal.

The profligate liberal and neo-liberal urban lifestyles of the late 19th and 20th centuries, may turn out to be a relatively short-lived phenomenon, because the fuel, water and breathable oxygen that maintain them is steadily running dry. These are factors that may prove to be not only a source of pain and suffering to humanity, but ultimately a liberating experience for human kind, reviving -through necessity- our human instinct to interact and cooperate, to share pleasure and pain, and to rebuild our broken communities.

The appropriate re-subordination of the oil and coal powered machinery which usurped the skilled application of human hands will remove one of man's main self imposed taskmasters; *but the real benefit will only occur if and when, we acknowledge just how and why we managed to construct a society with goals only attainable by first suppressing, and then divorcing ourselves from our fundamental social, spiritual and humanitarian instincts.* Not only this, but the lesson will have to be sufficiently imprinted on our brains to avoid making the same errors all over again.

To be social means to share: not as morality, but as a *response.* We are given something so we feel the desire to give something back. Once this instinct is subordinated by intellectual distancing or abstract material obsessions, we are no longer capable of acting as social beings, but only as antisocial automatons.

Modern day socialising is very different from a bonding experience borne out of shared work, directed towards a common goal. The latter produces a kind of blood tie between individuals that endures, whereas getting together in pubs and cafés, dinner parties or business meetings does not; it merely simulates the true experience. Sport, especially team sports, can induce bonding, but since the professionalisation of sports placed money ahead of the realisation of human skills, the motivation of both players and spectators has been distorted; often grossly. At least two zeros need to be wiped off top sportsmen's and women's salaries, to even begin to redress the absurd imbalances on display to-day. Better still, the return of all sports to the amateur status from which they so dramatically departed.

Only crises, it seems, bring significant numbers of people together today, either to fight against the destructive manifestations of global corporate control, or to struggle together to rebuild livelihoods destroyed by war or acts of nature.

Social and cultural expressions are essentially a force for good, especially when they are harnessed to an overall goal whose aim is the betterment of mankind. Positive international and intercultural relations can, and should, be the foundation for world peace and security, leading to the recognition of a one world sister and brotherhood, composed of thousands upon thousands of varied lifestyles, expressions and dialects. But before we can celebrate our differences, we have to recognise our sameness – the needs, hopes, aspirations that we have in common and need to help each other to realise. It is these hopes that will fuel the great changes that we must rise up to meet with open hearts.

"No man is an island entire unto himself" wrote the English poet John Donne. None of us can truly 'get what we want' in isolation from others.

☐One of us can find happiness without giving as much as we take and helping each other along the road of life. We are all closely interconnected 'social' beings, so we may as well celebrate our difference and our sameness simultaneously!

The new emergent social order will be built upon recognition of the fact that sharing is a positive and completely natural human instinct which, in contrast to the possessive and protective distortions to which we have become accustomed, gives meaningful expression to our collective solidarity.

The setting for the renewed expression of our collective

solidarity will be born from the best of the past coupled to the most appropriate innovations of today and tomorrow.

If we let them, our survival instincts will guide us back to a way of life we once abandoned in favour of the chimera of an unsustainable, insupportable and ultimately alienating, race for the spoils of wealth.

2. Money and Economics for the Benefit of All

As we witness the dissolution of supposedly 'safe' financial institutions at the hand of speculative predators given free rein by successive neoliberal governments it is difficult not to feel a sense of apocalyptic delirium in the air. Where will it all stop? And when it does, what will be left?

The simple answer is: we do not know and can only guess at what such a played-out endgame might look like. But provided our survival instincts are sharp enough to receive a signal, it is highly likely to be a hot telegram:

"Urgent: retrench your position. Take finance out of the current system now. Reinvest in human community enterprise at local level. Repeat at local level. Rebuild from the grass-roots."

But to see where it all started, we have to go back a long way and ask some pretty fundamental questions. Such as:

Did man make a mistake in creating coinage and paper money as a way of valuing goods? Looking back from the perspective of the 21st century, we might conclude that he did, so utterly distorted and so misused has this invention been over the past millennia.

However, it is the accumulation of wealth as an end in itself, not the existence of money per se, that lies at the root of the problem. The hoarding and flaunting of accumulated wealth serves to provoke jealousy and vindictiveness between those who have little and those who have a lot. A state of affairs which has been the catalyst of hundreds of wars, invasions and subsequent repressions of human liberty.

With the 'grand' accumulation of wealth comes the power to influence affairs of the state and other countries, an action which in turn provokes antagonism and retaliation.

Coinage, as a measure of wealth, came into being as a means of rendering simple bartering more flexible – and of giving fluidity to the means of exchange. Where one bushel of wheat could be exchanged for x weight of firewood, coins of a certain weight of base or precious metals could be exchanged in amounts that were deemed equal to the value of the wheat and firewood.

Through the domestication and penning of livestock, and through the cultivation of cereals some 8,000 years before Christ, one can recognise the early symptoms of the process of 'wealth accumulation' which was to become such a distorted force in Western societies later.

Hunter gatherers and nomadic peoples did not stay long enough in one place to hoard goods and animals, or stored supplies of food, water and building supplies: a process requiring more permanent human settlements. Nor, initially, were the various sizes of animal herds equated with economic valuations of power and superior social status, something else which became firmly established with the later development of permanent settlements.

However, as these more permanent settlements grew in size and number, so too did their citizens become more dependent on stored surpluses, leading to annual stocktaking valuations becoming more commonplace, as well as value judgements between the stock owned by one individual or tribe and another.

Later, the possession and hoarding of precious metals and stones conveyed upon the owner various degrees of social status; hoarding such minerals also provided security and power.

The formal establishment of banks and a commercial trading class in the late middle ages greatly hastened the development of a money based economy, introducing middlemen with no grounding in artisan skills, or any direct working connection with the raw materials of life. Instead, these new merchants traded goods produced by others in return for cash payments; an almost abstract form of survival compared to their agricultural and artisan forbears.

This new merchant class associated itself with a more urban outlook. When, in the 17th century, banks started the highly controversial practice of lending money at specific rates of interest to be paid by the borrower (known as usury[1]), a further level of complexity was added to the economic evolution of society.

Lending money at interest was a practice started by medieval gold merchants, who invented what is now called 'fractional reserve banking' by lending certificates against a gold reserve, held for their customers in bank vault deposit rooms. This practice was later to lead to a dangerous and virtually uncontrollable level of global monetary expansion. It established the rise of an ever more powerful elite club of financiers, who used money (borrowed from clients) to 'work the system' for their own advantage. This eventually lead to them taking a controlling influence over vast empires of wealth garnered at the expense of hard working, non-speculative citizens, who had often scrimped and saved to build a secure foundation for family life. *The collapse of sub prime mortgages in North American and European banking institutions is a direct repercussion of worldwide financier exploitation of usury, and inflationary monetary creation unpegged to the physical value of precious metals or other basic material necessities.*

---

1 Usury itself has much earlier origins, dating back to the time of Christ and before.

We can trace the line of these developments as stemming from the late medieval period, and moving into the 19th and 20th centuries. A time when economic power shifted from farmers, individual entrepreneurs, wealthy landowners, monarchs and aristocrats – to corporations and companies – established specifically to trade in ever larger volumes of raw materials, and needing to borrow money in order to expand these trades.

By the time of the Renaissance, banks, based in the capital cities of Northern and Southern Europe, duly became the lending houses for corporation and empire-building expansion, eventually turning in profits as great (if not greater) than the corporations to whom they lent their customers' savings.

This process of expanding corporate wealth shifted the responsibility for monetary management from the individual to a more 'impersonal' company of individuals, identified as a 'company limited by guarantee' or a 'corporation' run by an elected board. Members of this board increasingly had no experience of, or connection with, the means of production, and were therefore alienated from manual work and those who performed it. A widening and socially disrupting rift thus developed between 'directors' and 'workers' -a rift which remains firmly in place today in nearly all large corporations- and is reinforced by governments dependent upon corporate wealth to prime their political coffers.

The evolution of national and global economies is not an abstract process. It is a direct outcome of our human propensity for invention and change. However, from the outset, such qualities have been infiltrated and polluted by characteristics of greed, envy and exploitation, based upon a craving for the acquisition of disproportionate levels of power.

Through this process, the acquisitive desire for personal material wealth has broken the direct social and working relationship that individuals once shared with each other.

This has led to the point where today, different segments of society exist in varying degrees of competitive alienation from each other, while remaining dangerously abstracted from the simple needs of life.

Such alienation includes an inability to hear – and respond to – the ever greater cries of distress of our long suffering planet, scarred and wounded by this relentless march of greed and virtually unchecked environmental exploitation.

Planetary welfare has been critically poisoned by our obsession with extracting ever greater profits from an ever diminishing resource base. The wholly misguided, endlessly repeated mantra, that 'permanent growth' of national and global economies is an essential prerequisite of a stable society, enforces a completely wrong understanding of our relationship with the physical world.

By and large, the greater the growth rate of the economy, the greater the loss of global resources, the denser the pollution and the more compromised the overall environment. Attempts to control such rampant growth in economies failed securely to put the lid on pressures to achieve high gross national product returns to national economies. Consequently, every politician, banker and financier who wishes to retain his job, insists (with pathological determination) that without constantly growing national and global economies, the world would fall apart at the seams. *Whereas the truth is that the world is falling apart at the seams precisely because of the relentless pressures for constant exploitative economic growth.*

It is not economies that need to grow, but the diversity of our planetary flora and fauna, and the more equitable distribution of our common wealth. The biodiversity of the plant and animal kingdom has been imploding and regressing at a rate closely pegged to the rate of expansion, and exploitation, of global and domestic economies. They are absolutely interconnected phenomena. Thousands of biological species are being lost every year, including rare medicinal plants, due to the over extraction of the finite wealth of the planet, and the incremental knock-on effects that pollute, destabilise and ultimately destroy the gene pool upon which we all depend.

Money exists in order to support the expansive wealth and diversity of nature including, by extension, the non-monetary wealth of man. But the current reality places nature and man in direct opposition to each other, ensuring the unchecked suicidal rush to mine every last ounce of economically valuable mineral, soil, plant and water resource the planet still has left to offer.

The planet's finite resources are our most valuable inherited capital asset -a gift to be shared by all- and we are the long-term trustees of this gift. They are not something to be mined, processed and squandered on the production and purchase of commodities, the majority of which has no relationship with the real needs and necessities of mankind: a case amply demonstrated by our vast overflowing rubbish tips.

The competitive drive for financial 'profit' and 'growth' to which all other values have become subordinated, is largely a compensation for a disproportionate lack of human compassion and inner growth. It is an ego fuelled psychosis which has ended up polluting all the main arteries of the planet as well as undermining the social cohesion of communities and societies throughout the world.

In all situations where profit driven economic goals are considered paramount, those who are most deserving of support receive the least. For example, responsible farmers and fishermen, general manual workers, teachers, nurses and social workers. Whereas those who carry out services of secondary importance to society, such as lawyers, bankers, corporate executives, pop stars and sportsmen, receive the highest monetary rewards.

If one takes such a situation to its logical conclusion, there will soon be no farmers, fishermen or builders left to provide our essential daily needs – but there will be plenty of starving executives.

The global economy is built on the blood, sweat and tears of those who own almost nothing and who will be unlikely to become any better off as the result of their efforts to gain a little something. It relies on a barely disguised modern day form of slavery, in order to amass the obscene profits and bloated salaries of its proprietors.

Global weather disruption accompanies the rise of industrial and post-industrial global economies; it is symptomatic, and could hardly be otherwise, given the road we chose to go down – and the degree to which we elected to over exploit and defile the finite resources that fuel the global economy.

The national and transnational corporations which have come to dominate our lives are spectacularly destructive, encapsulating a psychopathic expression of human alienation from the environment, as well as from the plight of millions of fellow human beings. An overriding emphasis on the excessive hoarding of monetary wealth has caused mankind to become detached from reality – and ever more alienated from simple humanitarian instincts.

Today, according to the United Nations, some eight hundred million on our planet live below the official poverty line (earning less than one dollar a day); while two and a half billion live on the poverty line (earning approximately two dollars a day). This is a shocking situation. But it is rendered even more shocking by the fact that the tenth richest person in the world owns capital assets worth five times the Gross Domestic Product of the whole of Africa while many transnational corporations regularly turn around annual profits of two to three billion dollars.

Equally, money itself has lost touch with any connection it once had with the value of base and precious metals. Today, it has become as detached as its inventors, a 'virtual currency' linked only to degrees of debt and interest in the vast, impersonal and permanently shifting global economy.

It is absolutely imperative that we discover ways of taking control of our economies again and on a human and humane scale. We have no choice other than to support local and regional initiatives that are aligned with humanistic and generally progressive concerns.

The new economy will find expression in well thought-out measures – through ethical investments of a proper scale and proportion that channel funds and human creativity into projects for the common good of caring communities.

The promotion of economic systems that lead to gross differences in the purchasing power of different individuals, reflect a deeply anti social and selfish society. The first prerequisite for a balanced and stable society is for all the minimum necessities of human beings to be met, and for a closing of the ever widening wealth gap between 'haves' and 'have-nots'. The second, and equally important objective, is to foster a non monetary, common goal or ideal around which all people can unite. This is described further in the Chapter 9 - Art, Education and Spirit.

A just economic system is one which establishes the best means for as many people as possible to realise their potential, and helps to build the shared goal or ideal of a caring society. There are systems fitting this description operating in various pockets around the world, and there are many efforts being made by thoughtful, aspiring individuals, to form more caring, holistic communities, able to integrate these goals.

The rich diversity of creative expressions that emerge when citizens are encouraged, and given the means to be inventive and entrepreneurial, are highly significant indicators of a healthy society.

All economics should thus have the aim of stimulating and catalysing decentralised, self-supporting economic structures, that enable people to become more secure and more self-reliant. These must centre on the progressive realisation of our innate, but largely unexpressed, creative potentials.

All infrastructure should thus serve the purpose of helping humanity –and nature– to reach a healthier, more subtle and more dynamic state of self-realisation. All money, and all forms of taxation, should be utilised only towards the realisation of these ends.

Human happiness, at its deepest levels, expresses the joy of existence, the celebration of life in all its glorious diversity. Economies should serve the same ends, nurturing and developing systems that exist solely to drive this state forward, fuelling our journey towards a more harmonious state of co-existence with our planetary resources, and with each other; thus achieving an ever deeper expression of our true purpose here on earth. All other economic trends should be recognised as an aberration – and a highly destructive one.

Resolution:

1. Banking and business investment systems only work if they provide a benevolent form of support where it is most needed: improving the material foundation which helps close the gap between those who have, and those who do not have.

2. Taxation –which had its mediaeval origins in kings demanding payment from their subjects in order to raise instant armies– if it is required at all, should be highly visible. In other words, any money raised collectively over sustained period of time, must have a pre-agreed and visible end use. Citizens should contribute to improvements deemed agreeable by the community, rather than being coerced into paying for whatever is deemed necessary, by a small group of distant decision makers.

In order to avoid corruption and misuse, collective money rais-ing of this form will have to be conducted and the proceeds put into effect – within the same community. Where there is a need to support any centralised national or international institutions, this should be done separately. All money raised should only be invested in schemes that enhance beauty, social cohesion and basic human security.

3. Levies applied to income should be used to redistribute wealth so that communities can meet overall needs for shelter, food, water, clothing, medicine and education, with no one miss-ing out. Later, taking this further to enable a real quality of life to be experienced by all. Quality, in this context, means subtle, beautiful and spirit enhancing. NOT the accumulation of wealth for wealth's sake or for any other ulterior power related motives.

Our economic world is violently out of balance. Some 2% of the world's population earn far too much (some gro-tesquely so) and some 20% earn far too little. A situation that spans rank opulence and absolute starvation. This re-flects a gross distortion of the money supply and the equita-ble distribution of wealth.

Of the 2% who earn far too much, 'x' percent use their excessive wealth to control the 20% who earn far too little. There has to be a fundamental change to any system that condones this sort of distortion. Quite obviously, this is not going to be possible via a top down resolution at this point in history. *Such a change therefore has to be put into effect at the local level, where its results can be observed, monitored and reported further afield.*

Cooperative approaches, using pooled local resources di-rected towards commonly embraced community goals are the way forward.

In order to transition towards an initially small scale economic revolution, from where we are now, it will be necessary to make some bold decisions. These can start by choosing carefully how we bank, invest and spend our money. The mainstream banking system (if there still is one by the time you read this book!) will put our money into the arms trade, genetic engineering corporations, nuclear power – or whatever is likely to show the greatest return at any particular time. Our planetary resource base is thus steadily exploited, by purely profit motivated uses of our money.

To avoid this, we must shift our cash reserves into ethical and morally responsible businesses and institutions that support wholly appropriate, sustainable and environmentally friendly enterprises. Enterprises that do not seek profit as their primary motivation, but nevertheless expect some return on their investment. Need instead of Greed.

There are now many such ethical banks and co-operatives that are leading the way in this new humanised form of investment. However, a word of caution here: the portfolios of institutions promoting 'socially responsible investment' have to be carefully researched before a decision is made. Some fall very wide of the mark in an effort to increase returns.

We cannot afford to live schizophrenic lives, at some point we have to put our money together with our beliefs and conscience. (See also Chapter 13-Government, Corporations and Globalisation)

In many circumstances, money does not need to be used as the main form of exchange. Instead we can barter and swap one sort of goods for another. This process has a number of advantages over money exchange, particularly at the community level, where it builds on local skills and develops trust and social intercourse among a wide range of individuals.

How we spend our disposable income is obviously equally significant. As with conscious banking, so conscious shopping. The more continuity we can bring into our lives, the greater influence will we exert on society. Therefore, to purchase thoughtfully, in the spirit of an informed and discerning individual, is a very different thing than purchasing purely for 'convenience'. Buying from a person or business that you consciously wish to support is vastly better than buying only on price and convenience. The former is socially positive act, while the latter is largely selfish act.

However this does not apply to situations where earnings are insufficient to allow for altruism. Here, it is the task of society as a whole to reduce significantly the earnings gap between different strata of society, so everyone can afford to make simple, responsible choices, and no one is ultimately excluded from such a fundamental human right.

3. Technology and Science – for Life

Both technology and science carry the potential to greatly advance or significantly retard man's evolution, as well as that of the planet. In too many cases both started out with good intentions but ended up producing disastrous results.

It is only by learning from past mistakes that we become more discerning about the way we build, handle and apply all forms of science and technology in the future. Glorifying our scientific and technological achievements, without admitting just how drastically we have misused their potentials, is a fruitless and misguided form of self deception. Yet dismissing them out of hand is equally misguided.

What forces have been driving developments in technology over the millennia?

Clearly man has, since the beginning of settled human existence, been singularly devoted to finding mechanical and technical means to free himself from burdensome work loads. The industrial and agricultural revolution would not have been possible without an accompanying will to find 'technological solutions' to ease the manual labour load. But, for those who instigated the dramatic changes, it was not free of being tainted by a desire for profit and control.

Man's ingenuity and technical prowess greatly predates the 18th century industrial revolution. The invention of our first tools for splitting wood and digging the earth are already examples of such invention; as was the building of the first wheel during the Sumerian age – a 'revolution' if there ever was one! Each represented a major breakthrough in the technological innovation of emerging societies.

At that stage, such advances made little impact on the environment, and did not unduly scar the earth's surface. Early man's quest for more mobility and better tools for shelter construction and food growing found expression in small scale production units, usually directly attached to the home. But as populations increased and tools got bigger and more sophisticated, the new technologies started to dominate; shifting the work load more quickly and with less and less direct human connection with the earth's minerals and soils. A new love affair with mechanisation was emerging, and, for better or for worse, the old 'bond of nature' was being loosened.

These new technologies also became the source of power and control for those who owned them; opening up a growing schism between the simple work force and the increasingly aloof wielders of these technologies.

The technology of aggression and protection also took on a new significance. Once fixed human abodes (in contrast to hunter gatherer nomadic ways) became established – so was the need to defend such communities against invasion by others. Good 'defences' thus became a real concern, and the technology associated with both attack and defence grew more sophisticated.

Once full-scale wars started to be waged between rival tribes, and later, provinces and countries, the weapons of war became increasingly decisive to the outcome. The contribution of technology and science to the development of the weapons of war thus equals that of the development of tools for delivering necessary food, fabric and manufactured outputs.

It is noteworthy that the arms industry today stands amongst the highest export earners of many post-industrial economies, led by the UK. War, it seems, has been big business for a long time.

During the industrial revolution, resources were poured into the factories and special machines were built to mass-produce the basic material needs of society. Steel, heated and moulded by coal-fired furnaces, quickly forged a new relationship between man and the material world, and an increasingly drastic one. Serious factory based atmospheric pollution became a problem for the first time, as more and more people moved into towns and cities seeking wealth and opportunity. The bourgeoisie, that grew up in the emerging affluent urban and suburban communities, increasingly surrounded themselves with manufactured 'things', announcing an age of affluence, surplus and luxury – at least for those who owned and controlled the technology.

The process that enabled this 'luxury living' to become realised was pivotal, because it validated a lifestyle which was to prove unaffordable and unsustainable in the longer term. Industrial capitalist societies broadcast a signal to the rest of the world that it is OK to live off the planet's mined finite capital resources – as though they were infinite. They demonstrated that to 'live beyond our means' is the prerogative of those who can afford it. Ever since then, the rest of the world has been rushing to catch up, so as to also enjoy the spoils of the world's mined capital assets – before they run out.

It has been a desperately irresponsible role model to hold up to the 'non-developed' world, who are not now going to voluntarily give up their chance to cash in on the chimeric bonanza, in spite of the fact that it would take at least five more worlds to provide the resources necessary to enable all peoples of the planet to achieve post-industrial Northern European and North American standards of 'unsustainable living'.

How about science?

Science in its pure and unpolluted form is a dynamic search for the origins of life, a process of building conscious awareness of the working mechanisms of universal and planetary forces. The further science goes in uncovering and naming the building blocks of life, the further is our (rational) knowledge base increased; but this does not mean that we fully comprehend what it is we have discovered or what to do with this knowledge. For example, once it was discovered that the process of splitting the atom produced exponential increases in energy, the question of whether and how to exploit this energy took on as much significance as the discovery itself – or at least, should have.

Science and technology came together at much the same time. In many ways they were, at the early stages, indivisible. When man started gauging distances between two places and adopting measurements and a sense of proportion – he was already utilising a form of terrestrial scientific evaluation. An observation of the sky and the changing positions of the sun, moon and stars brought a new level of macrocosmic scientific awareness into being.

By the time the pyramids were being constructed (circa 2,000 BC) in ancient Egypt, architecture, science and technology had all found an interrelated expression. And because of developing skills in language and writing, mankind gave names to these pursuits, separating the one from the other and starting the process of specialisation and what we call 'professional expertise'.

For example, chemical experiments, to find out what happened when two or three basic elements were mixed together, were soon followed by the first attempts to prove the existence, dynamics and properties of matter as well as the composition of non-visible, atmospheric properties.

Science rapidly spawned many different branches, from astronomical observation to the advent of medicines and specialist engineering. They in turn gave birth to a whole raft of other specialist skills, leading to the vast plethora of 'scientific' specialisations we find today.

But as with all advances, the pure research soon became polluted with 'ulterior motives'. In the scientific arena – and in the advanced world of technology – the temptation grew to start manipulating life forces and natural elements for ends other than those which enhance man's well-being or greater knowledge.

The early alchemists tried to make gold from base metals, so as to acquire instant wealth and prestige. Advanced weapons designed to wipe out large numbers of fellow human beings soon found a ready market, and their inventors were eager to earn profits from their sales.

Controversy was rife during mediaeval times in Europe, as the new world of scientific enquiry produced ideas that clashed with entrenched church doctrines centred on 'flat earth' theories. When Copernicus and later, Galileo (1564-1642) pronounced that the world was not situated at the centre of our universe, but rather the sun was, the Church tried to ridicule and persecute them for so brazenly contradicting the prevailing Catholic doctrine.

However, such fundamental astronomical discoveries had a greater significance. Not only did they discern an elliptic structure of our universe, they also implied that when something sets out on a journey, the ultimate destiny is always the starting point. Columbus, sailing off towards the horizon, did not fall off the end of the world, as some had confidently predicted he would.

Copernicus and Galileo's observations, which had been

superseded by much earlier (non-European) civilisations, also lead to the hypothesis that the repercussions of all actions must return to the initiators.

The birth of awareness of cause and effect was coming into being, and with it, comprehension of the fact that we live in a round world –not a flat one– together with a first scientific glimpse of the cyclic forces behind the decay and rebirth of all biodegradable matter, the indivisibility of the cycle of nature, the celestial orbits of planets and stars and even the existence of memory.

However, the western world wasn't ready for such a broad comprehension of the nature of our universe. Further scientific endeavours were needed to put together the missing pieces of the puzzle. Sir Isaac Newton (1642-1720), the acclaimed British scientist, was to take just such a step, causing another great scientific stir by opening up a new world of understanding with his "laws of motion" and "laws of universal gravitation"; thus giving birth to the world of theoretical physics and a first understanding of the principles behind the universal movements of objects.

But none of this prepared the (western) world for the startling scientific observations of Charles Darwin and the lesser celebrated Alfred Wallace. In the mid 19th century, Darwin's "On the Origin of Species" announced that 'natural selection' and not 'preordained order', was responsible for the evolution of the plant and animal kingdom. This was something of a bombshell, particularly for the Church, which, up until this time, had held that only God's decrees were behind all changes on our planet and beyond and that only heretics questioned this truth. The doctrines of the Church (until then considered the undisputed authority on the natural world) were beginning to lose ground and a new spirit of scientific enquiry was gaining momentum.

Albert Einstein, the great quantum physicist, and other probing scientists of the late 19th and 20th centuries, succeeded in moving such scientific enquiry into the realm of a deeper universal awareness, pointing to further recognition of our inherent interconnection with the forces of nature. Man, it was posited by the poet John Donne, is not "an island entire unto himself": a state which Newtonian physics had tended to confer upon the universe; seeing the great orbs that move through space as a clockwork and generally mechanistic unchanging parade.

Einstein and Donne, in a crossover of science and poetry, increasingly saw man as an integral part of the very landscape and universe which more reductionist scientific opinion observed as separate, and somehow beneath the more 'lofty' and aloof human position. Thus, the torch lit by Copernicus, Galileo and some latter-day scientists, was picked up and carried forward into modern times; all the while expanding in its scope to spread greater knowledge and a broader comprehension of life's mysterious workings.

However, if earlier recognition of the significance of our planet's round shape and position within the universe had truly taken root in society as a whole, rather than being pigeon-holed as something of largely scientific interest only, our world might have been spared the fearsome wounds inflicted on her over the past millennium.

It has been a small, but highly influential club, that has (since the Middle Ages) been determined to utilise science and technology as a means to flatten out and to dominate, rather than nurture and enhance, the cyclic laws of nature. The present state of our planet is proof of their misguided success.

Today, we see much of science and technology reverting back to the flat earth principles that are supposed to have been left far behind. Linear thinking and 'technical fixes' are still heavily relied upon as the main hope for getting us out of the mess we caused by their earlier misapplications.

We cannot even begin to count the cost of having invested so much blind faith in the tools of our technological wizardry: but we are now experiencing these costs, and our naivety, first hand. *Only a quantum shift of consciousness away from reductionist, monocultural obsessions of the mind, can bring about the new direction required: a holistic grasp of our absolute interrelationship with all life forms.*

Those who claim that only a technological solution can secure society's future needs are failing to grasp the multidimensional nature of the task at hand. The proponents of a nuclear power panacea for electricity generation belong to this category. As with the genetic engineering of our food supply, nuclear proponents see the world through double skinned laboratory lenses and fail to face up to the evidence – including the thousands of Chernobyl deaths – that reveal the true price of converting finite uranium resources into highly carcinogenic radioactive substances with a half life of up to thirty thousand years. Just as the proponents and creators of genetically modified organisms fail to admit that their inventions cross contaminate and pervert the DNA of long-established plants, seeds and animals.

What right does one generation have to leave such a toxic and denatured legacy for future generations to cope with?[2]

Throughout history, every inventive first step taken by man has somehow been corrupted or allowed to run out of control, catalysing an equally destructive repercussion. And each time we have failed to learn from our ever more costly mistakes.

As the rate of developments in the fields of science and technology has speeded up, so the repercussions have become more and more stark and more drastic. Now in the early years of the 21st century we are close to the point of being able to artificially recreate almost every element of

---

2 It seems likely that the obsession with nuclear power is more closely associated with the perceived need for a stockpile of military fissionable 'weapons grade' materials than for civil energy concerns.

life. Such a bizarre techno-science is needed – according to genetic engineering specialists, nano technology exponents and pharmaceutical laboratory directors – to counteract the fact that we have rendered our world almost uninhabitable to sentient mortals. We have so polluted our natural environment and so distorted our foods through pesticide applications, genetic manipulation and over-processing, that some believe the only resort left to mankind is to genetically modify ourselves, so as to be able to stay alive on a planet many of whose main organs have come close to being damaged beyond repair.

It is an extraordinary indictment of grandiose human folly to have arrived at such a crassly stupid state of existence. While the will to live is a powerful instinct, a robotic genetically engineered human race is a self-defeating and utterly sterile expression of our human potentialities. Is this really what our Creator had in mind for us?

Our task, and a central tenet of *Renaissance 21*[3], is to recognise the existence of these trends, but to firmly and swiftly reject them. We need to take control of our destiny and rid the world of such malevolent and sterile 'flat earth' technologies. This means adopting and inventing those technologies that do not, or only the absolute minimum, harm to nature and to man.

The famous technological entrepreneur, Fritz Schumacher, author of *Small is Beautiful*, proposed an Intermediate Technology as the best way forward. He recognised the need to create affordable tools that feel good in human hands and that are of a scale appropriate to our human physique, gender and particular environment. They should, he said, possess the characteristics of smallness, simplicity, affordability and non-violence.

Since Schumacher's death in 1977, the development of

---

3 Renaissance 21 is the name I have given to the process of change we need to bring about.

some of the alternative renewable energy technologies that he advocated has gathered pace; but all too often the scale is not *small*, nor capitally cheap – and could not be described as non violent.

The appropriateness of *scale* has been forgotten in the rush to cash in on the new 'renewables' market. A rush that bears all the hallmarks of a new industrial revolution, with many of the same resource mismanagement implications.

If we are to avoid getting sucked into a 'green' commercial race for power, we will have to regroup, reconsider, and gain a proper understanding of the true way forward.

In 2008, it will be technically possible to draw the majority of all our household and small scale industry energy needs from a combination of solar, wind, water, biomass, geothermal and bio-digester methane sources. Aside from these, a whole raft of other renewable energy resources will soon be at our disposal, and there should be nothing to stop us designing systems that harmonise our inventions with subtle planetary forces that we have largely ignored until now.

It is both perfectly possible, and definitely desirable, to find just the right scale of development and design for each and every bioregion of the planet. *However, it is crucial to recognise, that this will only be possible in decentralised, community based population centres, where the technology is owned by the people and not by profit driven corporations.*

As people once again return to the land, labour saving solutions will no longer be the main focus. Labour enhancing ones however, will. It heralds a time of great inventiveness and imagination. A time to put all our skills and energies towards giving back to life that which we took (and misused) over the course of history. A time to work *with*, rather than *against*, nature.

This applies to all shelter and industrial construction and all agricultural work. To architecture, design, building, transport and engineering, communications and broadcasting technologies. We will be pushed into taking this route even if we do not voluntarily elect to go down it, because 'nature's revolt' will finally cut off and destroy the global economy, rendering us incapable of living off what remains of the overmined wealth of our long suffering world. This time is at hand.

Recommendations:

1. *All technological and scientific developments should be directed towards harmonising and enhancing man's relationship with nature, the cosmos and with fellow men: with no exception.*

2. *Wherever technologies exist that cannot be comprehended by ordinary people or cannot be constructed by simple skilled labour, they should, in almost all circumstances, be considered inappropriate and be systematically dismantled.*

3. *In keeping with point 1, all technologies that are large scale, centralised, and beyond the control of ordinary citizens should be reevaluated in the context of the change-over to regional and local resource based 'humanised' technologies. Electricity generation through one centralised grid should be deconstructed to allow for localised energy loops circulating locally produced renewable energy. As with food under 'The Proximity Principle' (see Agriculture and Environment) so with energy. Only surplus regional generation should be exported to the nearest undersupplied region.*

4. *Science and Technology should serve to fulfil the need for ecologically sensitive 'light footprints' and human scale developments that enhance every individual's sense of self esteem and participatory involvement in shaping developments in the chosen area of settlement.*

5. *Developing new technologies should be a fun and creative experience, a direct extension of a child's imagination flow and an inquisitive exploration of the laws of cause and effect. This way we will build warm humanity into machines and tools that can otherwise become burdensome, unappealing and ultimately destructive.*

6. *Tools and technologies are an extension of man, not man an extension of tools and technologies. We must never allow ourselves to be subjugated to a sense of impotence by our own inventions. Nor must those inventions ever be used to subjugate others.*

7. *Within the context of misguided uses of science and technology, the construction of weapons and instruments of war (whether on the ground or in space) and the trading of these for profit is an abhorrent human activity and must be swiftly curtailed.*

8. *In choosing what materials to use in order to meet the genuine needs of society, one must always look to utilising local, renewable materials first. Only when these are unavailable is it permissible to utilise some materials from further afield. And only as a last resort, in exceptional circumstances, utilising mined and refined non-renewable materials whose manufacture causes damage to the environment. Character in buildings is reflected in the local materials used in their construction.*

9. *In respect of our planet's ecology, we need to plan the future of our communities holding in mind the image of a dynamic village community. In such a community bicycles and good shoes are more important than cars. Connections with other communities, towns and cities are better achieved by railway, canal, river or horse, than by motorways. In the fields and woods that supply our village with food and fibre, horses work more effectively than petroleum-hungry tractors. In the new houses needed for village residents or newcomers, ecological houses made from clay and straw,*

adobe or local stone and wood are better than those made from mass produced bricks and concrete or wood from unsustainable mining and forestry enterprises.

10. Microchips for computer software or photovoltaic panels will have to be produced in ways which do not pollute the environment or utilise excessive natural resources. Similarly, electro magneticmicrowaves, mobile phones and their transmitter masts, plus many other microwave-dependent technologies, lead to the creation of "electrosmog" which weaves a dangerous blanket of microwaves around our planet – disorientating man and animal alike. According to independent research microwave transmissions (civil and military) are altering global and local weather patterns. This may also play a role in 'colony collapse disorder' among bees through disruption of the earth's magnetic field emissions, used by birds and insects to gauge their flight patterns. Further research in this field is vital.[4]

11. Animal cloning experiments, genetic engineering, nanotechnology and all experiments that involve attempting to alter the gene pool of life in order to profit from it, have no place in a society dedicated to rebalancing and renurturing the common life force, which is perfectly capable of sustaining us all, when properly cared for.

12. Ultimately, individuals will become so attuned to the environment in which they live and through which they move, that no harmful technologies will be tolerated. The earth, man and the universe will be understood to be one unified, sensitised being, with an infinite number of subtle colours, hues and expressions. Our own contribution in shaping the beauty and health of this Great Being will be seen to be as significant the as Great Being's contribution to shaping and moulding us. Darwin and the Church

---

4 Recommended reading "Owning the Weather", Prof. Michel Chossudovsky, Foundation for Global Research.

need argue no more: Responsibility will be shared equally and joy-fully.

4. Agriculture, Environment and Rural Economy - the Foundations of Human Survival

"Treat the Earth well, it was not given to us by our parents, it was loaned to us by our children." Kenyan proverb

Agriculture literally means 'a culture of the field'. That already says a lot about how far removed from their roots, the current 'factory farming' mass produced food systems that feed most of the developed world, really are. It also shows how impoverished we are, as are our soils, as a result of reducing much of agriculture to nothing more than another industrial conveyor belt. So exploitative has industrial agriculture been over the last century that more than forty per cent of the world's soils have become drained of fertility and are now incapable of food production without the application of huge doses of agrochemicals. It is said that a civilisation which is losing its seeds and destroying its soil, is a dying civilisation: and we are. Today, over eighty percent of mankind's current diet is provided by the seeds of less than a dozen plant species – and most of those are 'owned' by just two or three transnational corporations. Ninety eight percent of vegetable varieties hasdisappeared from the western world over the past one hundred years. Unless this catastrophic loss of biodiversity is reversed, our gene pool upon which all life depends – will run dry within the span of this century.

According to "The Living Planet Report" (a UN and WWF International report reported in the Guardian October 29 2008) "Humans are using 30% more resources than the earth can replace each year, which is leading to deforestation, degraded soils, polluted air and water, and dramatic declines of fish and other species." "As a result" says the report "we are running up an ecological debt of four trillion to four and a half trillion dollars every year – double the estimated losses made by the world's financial institutions as a result of the credit crisis." This report also states that fifty countries are now experiencing moderate to severe water stress on a year round basis.

The way we manage our land and water is perhaps the best barometer of all for indicating the state of health (or sickness) of society as a whole. So fundamental is the production of food and the correct management of water to our survival and well-being, that they must be placed at the number one position in any society which is interested in its self-preservation and longer term sustainability. This must also include the management of woodlands and forests, often wrongly thought of (or compartmentalised) as less significant than the growing of food. Fibre and fuel are ultimately as important as food and water, and the way we utilise and manage our timber resources must share the distinction of being at the top of our list of survival priorities.

Agricultural and environmental concerns are so closely interrelated as to be almost indistinct from each other. The same can be said for the way in which we should approach them – as intimately connected areas of concern. We are, after all, also a part of nature's intricate living pyramid, but having the additional special role of being key trustees of its long-term health and welfare. A trusteeship which has been largely ignored and abused over the millennia.

Environment, in its non-agricultural state, requires a different methodology, of course. Sometimes a completely 'hands-off' approach is best i.e. in the Arctic and the Antarctic. Otherwise, as in the case of wildernesses, national parks and special reserves, a 'managed' approach is necessary, but a subtle, thoughtful and caring hand must prevail, if these biologically rich zones are to be properly maintained in the long term.

Forestry and farming cross over in many instances. Running pigs in woodlands or grazing sheep in orchards are rather rudimentary examples. There are many medicinal and herbal plants, as well as edible fungi, that cross over and interconnect both environments, accompanied by native birds, insects and fauna. The 'good steward' of the land will always sense the intimate connection with and interconnection between the different facets that compose agriculture and 'nonfood' environmental management. The role of good stewards is to establish an ever more sensitive and dynamic interaction between the activities that provide the human need for food, fuel, fibre and water, and the long term health and welfare of the environment in which this process takes place. It is at once both an art and a science – and we who take on the trusteeship of this process, are eternal students, so much is there to discover and learn.

So, where did it all go so wrong?

It is possible to go back a long way in uncovering the symptoms of the current profound malaise of our natural resource base, due to the intense exploitation of soil, plant, animal and man. An exploitation so ruthless and so thorough, in most post-industrial 'developed' regions of the world, that the majority of top soils into which our seeds are now planted, are no longer able to support the desired plant growth without heavy doses of soluble synthetic nitrate fertilisers and accompanying pesticides. Sterile and dying soils are endemic wherever industrial agriculture has taken hold, with its systematic mononeutralisation of traditional rotational farming practices. Also, its indefensible imprisonment of millions of farm animals for the factory-style mass production of the 'cheap food' that lines the shelves of supermarket chains across the world. (See Chapter 8-Man and Animal)

Every country has a varying historical account of the pressures that shifted agricultural practices away from those based on returning organic matter to the soil, rotating crops and nurturing livestock. But in Europe, the advent of the Industrial Revolution, led by England in the 18th century, marked a major shift towards larger scale farming enterprises, designed to supply the rapidly expanding urbanisation process: a process that was itself fuelled by the unprecedented levels of employment needed to man the new factories and related downstream industries. A vast demographic 'country to town' shift was set in motion which is still continuing today. In fact in 2006, the numbers of people living and working in cities across the world, exceeded those living and working in the countryside for the first time ever. This in turn, has put unsustainable pressure on planet earth to provide for the needs of urban based populations.

The apparently irresistible urban generated economic stimulus that accompanied the industrial revolution, attracted already partly disenfranchised farm labourers and artisan craftsmen away from their rural communities and into a new life in the towns. With so many leaving the land, maintenance of the economic viability of the countryside increasingly depended upon a new breed of entrepreneur taking the helm, as well as new labour saving machines to replace the human hands now engaged in manning the grinding conveyor belts of the industrial revolution.

In the UK, *the Agricultural Enclosures Act of 1865 marked the final culmination of some two to three hundred years of forced ejection of the peasantry from once 'common' land.* It placed the wealth of this land in the hands of a small body of wealthy individuals, who retained very little interest in its long term ecological management; but a considerable interest in its ability to turn a good profit. Such motivation provided further impetus to the redefinition of the countryside as the domain of owner-occupier yeoman farmers and wealthy aristocrats often at least partly economically dependent on the fruits of the city. A new breed, who had a more detached connection and contact with the land than their farm working predecessors.

These new landlords' interests leaned towards novel farm animal breeding and crop improvement schemes, which included the laboratory development of faster growing, higher yielding cereals and grasses. These new techniques led to "hybridisation" of crops: high yielding seeds, cross-fertilised to produce greater yields, but often at the expense of disease resistance, flavour and nutritional content.

Under this new regime, the older, indigenous crop varieties, whose selection and breeding had followed a slower field based process of evolution, were steadily superseded. Agricultural productivity became more and more controlled from the laboratory – and the economic rewards were increasingly reaped by seed and plant breeders. They were soon to be joined by the agro-chemical pesticide companies, whose products were increasingly sought after, to prevent the new hybrids succumbing to diseases that had not affected their older, better adapted, cousins.

However, the greatest change was to come in the aftermath of the 20th century's two world wars, events that shook Europe to its foundations. The vast, war-inspired munitions industry, spawned by the demand for millions of bullets, shells and bombs, later became the source of synthetic soluble nitrate fertilisers and a new breed of pesticides: derivatives of the surplus nitrous oxides and nerve gas compounds stockpiled during World War II. A whole new package of synthetic, chemical components that were claimed to be essential for the successful establishment of a modern, profitable and efficient farming sector, were thus born: vastly speeding up the rate of destruction of native biodiversity, as well as traditional rotational farming systems.

The speed with which this 'brave new world' of synthetic input farming swept aside more traditional practices was nothing short of astounding. Synthetic chemicals, dependent upon cheap oil for their production, rapidly displaced farmyard manures and clover leys, as the main means of providing quick acting phosphate, potash and nitrogen to the soil. An exponential increase in the use of synthetic pesticides, herbicides and fungicides quickly followed suit, as a necessary adjunct to prevent the weakened nitrogen forced crops from succumbing to air and soil borne diseases.

For the first time, governments started talking about farming as an "industry", tailored to a highly mechanised, low labour, industrial style mono-cultural mass food production system. The new breed of post World War II farmer was encouraged to develop the skills of a businessman, and work tirelessly to make his enterprise efficient and profitable, fit to supply the emerging development of an economically valuable world export market.

Only a handful of farmers in the UK defied this rush into chemically dependent food production, in which a degree in chemistry and business management became as, if not more important, than the well honed skills and land based knowledge of the farmer.

In the UK, a small group of such farmers, committed to best practice rotational mixed farming systems, came together in 1946, and, with a few respected progressive soil scientists, nutritionists and doctors, formed the Soil Association: an organisation whose declared aim was to carry forward research and development into ways of maintaining and increasing soil fertility through applying an ecologically sound agricultural practice and appropriate crop and animal rotations around the farm.

Eve Balfour (the founder) and her colleagues, served warning on mankind that the foundation of natural bio-diversity was gravely threatened by the rapid move into agrochemically assisted monocultural farming systems. This auspicious affiliation of like-minded individuals, from different, yet connected, professional backgrounds, led later to the establishment of the land management system known as 'organic farming'. A stern warning was hereby offered to the world: *continue to destroy the biodiversity of the planet through taking agrochemically aided monocultural short cuts to time honoured, sustainable systems of food production and one will land up starving all living beings to death.*

As we move on into the first decade of the 21st century, mainstream agro-chemical dependent food production systems have increasingly shown the symptoms Eve Balfour and her colleagues had warned of. Chemically treated soils are no longer producing annual rises in cereal and grass yields, instead they are showing all the symptoms of steril-ity. Their nutrients are running at such depleted levels, that soluble artificial replacements now have to be added to the list of sprays regularly applied to the starved land. In short: farming systems have become even further alienated from their origins.

A powerful lobby of transnational seed and agro-chem-ical corporations have teamed up to establish a controlling influence within the globalised food, seed and animal feed industry of today, with direct links to government institu-tions and large supermarket chains. The European Union's Common Agricultural Policy plays along with this corpo-rate power base. It ensures that eighty per cent of agricul-tural subsidies go to just twenty per cent of the farmers: the largest and most exploitative operators.

Native seeds, expropriated from the peasant farmers who nurtured them over the centuries, are now genetically "re-designed" and patented by these same, increasingly predatory corporations. These genetically modified seeds are then sold back to the struggling farmers, whose original 'intellectual property rights' (homegrown seeds) had already been covertly abducted. But they can only purchase them as part of a package, which includes specific agro-chemicals designed to be used in tandem with the sowing of these new 'novel' seeds. What is even worse, the farmer is forbidden to save the resulting harvested seeds for his/her own use – a time honoured practice throughout the world, crucial to the subsistence of hundreds of millions of smallholders. Instead, the farmer must sell them back to the GM seed provider and pay an annual royalty fee for the right to purchase the next instalments.

It is hard to imagine a more extortionate way of profiting by others' innocent lack of awareness, yet the genetic modification of our seeds and foods, praised by government leaders and academic researchers, is simply another manifestation of a deeply flawed system which mercilessly exploits the profligate, unrestrained mining of our finite planetary resources. These are the latest laboratory contributions to a long line of technical fixes that have steered artificial input farming practices into a virtual reality world of alienation and abstraction from the native wisdom they so blithely dismiss.

Massive damage to the delicate productive fabric of our planet has been the now undisguiseable result. The ingestion of all artificially force-fed foods – including GM foods and foods which have been subjected to irradiation technologies cannot ensure the proper sustenance of human and animal health. However, they can lead to the rapid growth of a range of sometimes fatal illnesses and a severely compromised human immune system. Many of these human health problems are virtually untraceable to their sources, so profligate is the denaturing of our natural diet. The same applies to damage done to the entire gene pool upon which life on earth depends.

A turning point?

Now that most of the 'food' resulting from this process is being slowly recognised as nothing more than a pale imitation of the genuine article, we can assume that the time is ripe for a renaissance of fresh, local, seasonal and flavourful farm produce! The totalitarianism of homogenised, sterilised and utterly bland dairy, vegetable, meat and grain products is simply a mirror of the production systems that grow and process them. They are two halves of one abysmal whole; proudly washed, polished and tenderised for our instant consumption by the cling-filmed hands of the hypermarket global food giants.

Agricultural production and environmental care, as has already been said, are inherently inseparable. Leading on from this recognition, let us also include human, animal and indeed all living beings' health and welfare as being equally part of the same inherently interconnected process. Lady Eve Balfour, observed that the health of Soil, Plant, Animal, and Man is an inherently inseparable part of one dynamic cycle. Once any link in the chain is broken (or denatured) all other components are obviously also affected, or should we say 'infected'. This is such a fundamental principle that it deserves special cognizance, informing as it does, the very essence of a true understanding of how terrestrial elements interact and affect each other within the constantly evolving chain of life.

Quite simply, our farming must fully adhere to this sound ecological principle if we are to nurture our degraded soils, food, flora and fauna back into a truly 'living' condition.

This is the work which lies ahead of us, and it is a unique challenge upon the creativity and courage of humankind successfully to set in motion the complete transformation of current desensitised, destructive food production systems, and the by now sterile soils that support them. Only human scale, ecologically sound farming systems can feed our world and reward the often unrecognised skills of practitioners.

It is not a question of 'going back to nature'. It is a question of whether we want to retain enough independent food security to determine our own future, or to usurp that independence to those who will decide our future for us.

Food sovereignty, worldwide, currently rests upon the support and maintenance of environmental friendly family farming traditions. Family farming, in most countries, is largely a peasant driven occupation and encompasses time honoured sustainable practices. It accounts for approximately 2.8 billion people, or close to fifty per cent of the world's population (FAO statistics). Its main characteristics include a focus on producing food for direct human consumption rather than for anonymous market places, as well as a wider diversity of products rather than large monocultural concerns. Family farms are mostly mixed farms that favour a symbiosis between livestock rearing and cereal and fruit and vegetable production.

Enormous pressures for the liberalisation of the global economy have worked against this largely sustainable model of local food production. Deregulation of the market place and low investment have combined to drive some 60,000 farms out of business every year, according to the global peasant farmers' association Via Campesina. With their departure goes the ability for countries to feed their own people and an increasing dependence upon constantly fluctuating export markets often thousands of miles away.

Distortions in such trading practices are practised by all the world's main trading blocks. For example, the European Union insists on maintaining tariffs against cheap imports from third world countries while simultaneously insisting that these same countries maintain unrestricted markets for subsidised EU imports. EU products are then dumped on these countries, undermining their internal markets and destroying the livelihood of farmers depending on getting a fair (but usually very low) price for their locally traded produce. Such an iniquitous position undermines attempts to meet everyone's basic needs in a fair and sustainable manner. It also runs directly contrary to international laws on human rights, particularly the International Protocol on Economic, Social and Cultural Rights (1966).

The European Union's Common Agricultural Policy must be reformed to be based on the principles of food sovereignty, supporting farmer-based ecologically and environmental friendly agricultural systems that are compatible both with the needs of European farmers and with those of third world farmers. All countries must radically redress their policies to ensure that their citizens have fair access to locally and regionally grown foods, fuels and building materials – and are not left to fend defenselessly for themselves in a speculative, exploitative and intrinsically unstable global casino. Family farms still remain our best model for ensuring a sustainable food supply.

But farming should not be isolated from its inherent connection with social and cultural expressions. Little green shoots of activity centred around the integration and interweaving of cultural, social, economic and agronomic concerns are emerging all over the world. A Culture of the Field cannot only be about the science (or art) of sustainable land management; it must also express another dimension that integrates, and gives human expression to the reason why we would set about growing food at all.

Not so long ago, this sort of activity centred around the ritual feasts and celebrations of the annual harvest, the winter and summer solstices, and the main religious festivals. Nowadays these outbursts of exuberant thanksgiving and merrymaking have been sanitised and rendered largely inert, in much the same way as have our land and food. The blood relationship with the land and seasons that led to the description of farming as a 'way of life', has been thinned out and diluted, to such an extent that the emotional condition necessary to drive a proper seasonal celebration is no longer in circulation. Our bubbling red corpuscles and bucolic laughter have been consigned to the 'rare breeds' museum, along with our once multifarious farm animal breeds that bore witness to the jovial scenes.

Reintegrating cultural and artistic expression into ecologically balanced agricultural cycles will transform the way we experience the (sometimes onerous) daily tasks of the farming calendar. Youth will be attracted back to the land, realising that good parties are not the sole prerogative of the urban jungle. Imaginative young energies are now badly needed to invent and construct alternative human scale tools; a very necessary innovation in order more subtly to work the land. They are equally needed to develop the energy and transportation renewable technologies, essential to help countryside communities establish their own self autonomy and independence.

Food and energy security at the parish level must be the first objective. But as parishes overlap and interconnect with each other, so can the ideas, skills and resources of their citizens. We must NOT advocate an isolationist policy or attitude, as this contracts, rather than expands, our generative and imaginative qualities, as well as our natural social urge to share and learn with and from each other for the better of the whole.

Once a parish semi-self autonomy has developed an equilibrium and relative subsistence capability (food and energy security), then larger areas, defined as 'districts', can become resurrected as areas of geographical and bioregional significance and importance, as opposed to the purely administrative zones that identify them today.

In the 19th century, England's counties and districts had very individualistic characteristics. For example, there were different designs of plough to suit the different soil types, different breeds of cows, horses and sheep adapted to the varying indigenous flora and altitudes; even different accents and behavioural patterns between those living in adjoining districts.

As the 'localisation' process gathers pace, we will surely rediscover regionally characteristic archaeological evidence of forgotten resources, helping to point the way towards the availability of local building materials that give character and good adaptive strengths to houses and small scale industrial constructions. Likewise, regional medicinal and food providing plants and trees will reemerge, to become key components of the diets of citizens living in the areas where such plants become reestablished.

All efforts must be made to rebuild and maintain truly *local economies*. The income and resources generated must not be casually siphoned off into the broader economy, but be circulated at the local level, steadily building the strength of the community and making it possible to acquire improved conditions for the provision of all the necessities of daily life.

This in turn, will lay the foundation for the cultural, artistic and spiritual aspirations that bring to life, and give colour and character to communities, villages and townships.

Those who work the land and produce the cereals, dairy products, fruits, vegetables, meat and timber products, must also have a stake in the control of the processing plants necessary to turn these products into the foods we eat – or planks and beams we build with. This is essential in order to prevent outside bodies or middlemen from distorting local economies, and introducing selfish profit motivated goals that pollute the original aims and purposes. Here, cooperative efforts will be required. However, individuals have to first share the same commitment towards a common purpose before the bond that leads to true trust can be established – and the cooperative spirit is able to manifest itself.

Many times, attempts at forming land-based cooperatives have failed, due to a lack of cohesion and the lack of a genuine common commitment towards the success of the enterprise. In countries where individuality has tended to be prized higher than collectivity, it is not the simplest thing to establish the discipline needed to develop a cooperative spirit and a real sharing. But without it, good work and positive energies eventually become dissipated, led astray by selfish motives.

Many traditional rural economies of the past were founded on a spirit of basic cooperation because the attraction of outside wealth was less pervasive, and private and public transport far less developed. *Money had to be generated within the community.* Whereas today the majority of people living in the European countryside have little or no interest in the self-sufficiency of the community they live in. Instead they commute, often hundreds of miles to find work and to earn their living: contributing in the process to high CO_2 levels and a distinctly stressful lifestyle. The inauspicious creation of dormitory towns has been a direct outcome of this restless lifestyle.

If the essence is the need for a definitive move away from a centralised and corporate monopolization of profit motivated energy generation, including the heavy distribution grids that can, in the event of severe weather, or at the flick of a switch, black out whole communities without prior notice or justification. Pluralistic and regionally adjusted, decentralised rural economies, need to be reestablished not only for local employment imperatives but also for, and by, those who feel identified with these communities. It must be a grass-roots led, bottom-up process of self-regeneration, a taking ownership of –and responsibility for– the shape and sociocultural development of villages, towns and rural settlements.

The threefold threat presented by depleted (or politically controlled) oil reserves, increasingly unstable political institutions and economies, and wildly fluctuating weather conditions, continue to point to the absolute necessity of adopting a completely transformed approach to the way we live. Now we have to 'make life happen' at the local level, rather than relentlessly chase its chimeric shadow around the globe, setting up vast competitive 'trading blocks' in the process.

All long distance transportation of food relies heavily on fossil fuels. A reliance that pollutes and destabilises the upper atmosphere, as well as causing irreversible damage to the terrestrial environment over which the global movement of goods passes.

Further, the over-packaging, refrigeration and sanitising of food contributes to the misuse of vast amounts of manufactured energy.

It would be easy to write a book about this subject alone (as others already have), so widespread is the abuse of our precious resources in the apparently insatiable pursuit of garnering a profit from the fruits of the land. At the end of the thousands of miles of tarmacadam motorways, especially constructed for the transnational movement of food and other domestic commodities, lies a supermarket, hypermarket or mega store.

If cathedrals stand as symbols of man's aspiration to a higher spiritual consciousness, hypermarkets are surely monuments of society's lowest level of material greed. While the farmers and factory workers who toil to provide the products that line their plastic shelves receive the absolute minimum economic reward for their labour, the hypermarkets boast huge profits and evermore grandiose expansion plans. So distorted is the scale and motivation of this form of trading –and so destructive to both human and environmental welfare– that any caring individual should find it abhorrent to carry on worshipping at this golden calf.

In a world where everything is subordinate to the Free Market, the superstores are indeed the gods. Their emissaries specifically include the World Trade Organisation, the World Bank, International Monetary Fund, the United States Food and Drug Administration and Department of Agriculture, as well as the dominant agro-chemical, genetically modified seed and food conglomerates. It is a club that knows no end in its ambitions to dominate and control global resources and international trade. A club that stands squarely behind the clinical cloning of farm animals and the genetic engineering, patenting and declared 'ownership' of our common genetic resource base, an ownership that was given primacy by the World Trade Organisation. Under the articles of agreement of the Codex Alimentaris of 1995 the food giants have increasingly gained unrestricted freedom to enter and exploit the seed markets of developing countries and have gained exclusive 'intellectual property rights' over thousands of plant varieties. Thus the international agro-industrial conglomerates –that directly and indirectly support the supermarkets– favour the widespread destruction of global biodiversity and the brutal appropriation of peasant farmers' indigenous and basic means of survival.

In order to reinforce the revival of appropriate scale, local rural economies that are the antithesis of this apocalyptically reductionist approach, we must stick to some important basic principles. These I have described in other publications under the heading the "Proximity Principle", a phrase coined to emphasise the need to create a reciprocal supply and demand chain within the immediate circumference of population centres. A system that ensures that full utilisation is made of the local resource base, before turning to areas further afield for the community's basic needs.

There are a number of simple steps to be put in place to achieve this:

Firstly; the town or village committee should do some simple calculations concerning approximately how much food, energy and building materials (fibre) are required to maintain the sensible needs of their community.

Secondly; farmers and local foresters should be approached in order to establish how much of this need can be supplied. Initially a round table discussion between all parties concerned can set the process in motion.

Thirdly; a contractual agreement should be established between the local farmers and local citizens (consumers). Preferably led by the local citizens, who will be able to tell the farmers approximately what volume of specific products they would like to have grown for them on an annual basis.

Fourthly: the economic return to the farmer must be fair, with no attempt made to exploit his or her labour or to use the threat of going elsewhere to buy cheaper food or commodities. In return the farmer must guarantee to use ecologically benign systems of agriculture, and to strive to produce good quality nutritious and flavourful foods that can be enjoyed by all. The same applies to foresters, who must adopt sustainable, environmentally sound practices of timber management. Both will need to save their seeds and swap them locally to perpetuate native diversity.

Fifthly; the means of transportation, display and sale of these goods must reflect the minimum use of non-renewable polluting fossil fuels and non-degradable packaging. This is fundamental and reflects the pride of place essential to any homogeneous community, as well as to broader environmental care.

Sixthly; the consumers and producers must not act like entrenched camps. There should be a sharing and mutual understanding of needs in recognition of the fact that good community care is a common responsibility and a rewarding process, in which everyone plays an important part.

Seventhly; cultural, spiritual and artistic expressions should be encouraged to flourish, particularly those that give expression and impetus to the evolving way of life of the community. Young and old alike should be involved and recognise the values of their respective talents and wisdom (see Chapter 10-Youth meets Wisdom). Rural communities all have the potential to be dynamic and colourful centres of life. Our world is composed of millions of such communities – even big cities are a composite of hundreds of interconnected communities or boroughs.

This is the way we should consciously see and design the world in which we live, because the scale, layout and visual beauty of our landscapes, villages, towns and working places must find harmony and resonate with our own sense of inner peace and security. The laws of man and the laws of nature must find themselves ever more closely intertwined, harmonised and mutually enhanced.

Eighthly; the Proximity Principle establishes a model which can be replicated right across the land, so that all villages, market towns and even larger towns refind their connection to the land upon which they were built – and reestablish their direct links with the surrounding landscape and natural resource base.

Market towns have a particularly important role to play here, as they were historically designed to attract trade to their central market places through a road system radiating out from the centre like spokes from the hub of a wheel. Their pedigree suggests that they should now become 'rural enterprise hubs', echoing anew their historical raison d'être and leading the way towards the development of thousands of similarly placed local economies. The widespread adoption of the Proximity Principle will ensure that local, fresh, seasonal quality food will be available to all citizens, not just a minority currently able to afford such produce.

Where the production of local food, fuel and fibre is insufficient to meet the needs of the community it connects to, then the nearest area with a surplus can make up the difference. Likewise, communities with considerable surpluses can be providers of adjacent under-supplied communities and so on, replicated throughout the country and monitored at the parish, district and county levels so as to fulfil the internal self-sufficiency and food, fuel and fibre needs of each region of the land. *Ultimately, only any national surplus or deficit will trigger an export opportunity or an import requirement.* But the random import and export of globally or inter-continentally traded basic commodities has no place in this system. It does not preclude the continued trading of products that are not what can be defined as 'staple needs', but it will cut out the appallingly wasteful practice of importing and exporting foods easily grown or raised in both countries of origin. Thousands of communities, all operating to the simple criterion of the Proximity Principle, can and will provide a major reduction in CO_2 emissions which simply cannot be successfully achieved in any other way.

It is a question of rehumanising our existence and renurturing our deeply wounded planetary health. It is only when we have created some momentum in bringing about these changes that we will be in a position to offer so-called 'Third World' countries a reasonable model to emulate. The practice of sending 'experts' to teach natives of less industrially developed nations how to repeat our own bad habits is one of the outstanding examples of post colonial arrogance still widely practised today. In fact, were we not so headstrong and so falsely sure of the innate superiority of our western ways, we would have long ago recognised that we had as much, if not more, to learn from the peasant farmers of the world than they have to learn from us.

This lesson will soon come home to roost, whether or not it is voluntarily absorbed. Most of what we call 'progress' and 'development' is essentially a profit motivated, blink-ered and completely unsustainable rush to cash in on the last ounce of available wealth still there to be stolen from unsuspecting communities across the world.

5. Climate and Consumers to Have or to Be?

Some things, it seems, are beyond our control, and this makes us feel rather frightened, because we are accustomed to order our lives according to a variety of 'almost certainties', that only vary slightly from day to day. We seek reassurance about the likely rises or falls of our investments, food and energy prices, temperature fluctuations, our personal health, safety and so on. However, we are generally not aware that what we were doing two hundred years ago, one hundred years ago, thirty years ago and yesterday, has an unseen but steady cumulative effect on our planet, continuing to produce change on another dimension from the one we are most concerned with in our daily lives.

So it is with climate. The effect of at least two hundred and fifty years of burning fossil fuels for energy to fuel our factories, heat our homes and run our transport systems has produced pollution of a widespread and largely toxic nature. Over time, this pollution has extended itself to our rivers, air and soils and has become steadily more apparent. Some remedial actions (but never enough) have been taken to try and counteract the most obviously affected areas. But it is only in the last decade that we have become aware of the knock-on effect caused by CO_2 and other noxious pollutants spilling into the upper atmosphere for two and a half centuries.

Our Earth is a living being, so there need be no surprises in recognising the fact that if one constantly feeds a living being a diet of toxic substances, it will eventually become seriously sick. Living beings often develop a fever when pathogens upset the rhythm of their systems, they also vomit up indigestible items that won't break down into normal wastes. So it is with our Planet Earth. She has been force-fed an indigestible, non-organic diet for a long time; with some organs of her body, such as the seas and forests, absorbing huge levels of indigestible carbons before finally showing signs of critical acidification.

Our living Earth also has her own clothes to protect her from malign influences, such as strong ultra violet rays, meteorite showers, and undue heat and cold. But even these clothes, the ozone layer, stratosphere and ionosphere, are now wearing thin and developing holes, because of the man-made synthetic chemical compounds and electromagnetic microwaves that have impregnated and fractured them.

So now our Earth has a severe fever, and we are suddenly rushing around with thermometers and exclaiming about the remarkable, and often drastic course this fever is taking. So hot, and then suddenly so cold, within such short spaces of time. Such intense sweats breaking out and then such long periods with almost no moisture at all. We read the papers and see on television that this is an unprecedented occurrence and that various conventions have been convened to try and coordinate efforts to bring these problems under control. We fear that time is short in which to secure this recovery, and that serious changes will have to be made to our profligate energy consumptive lifestyles, if our patient the ever 'patient' planet which is our home – is to be nursed back into a robust state of well-being.

And all this is true, as far as it goes. CO_2 and many other pollutants will have to be radically reduced within a decade to bring about the sort of cleansing required to rejuvenate our soils, air and water supplies. Yes, a grand detox is needed, but not just of the planetary arteries and atmospheres, *but also in almost every aspect of our current way of thinking and doing. 'Thorough healing' is a multidimensional, holistic task, it cannot be performed on one or two elements in isolation from the others to which it is connected.*

However, if we sit back and allow big business to take the helm of this process of change, the ship will surely be set on a course which is more about profiting from big 'green' contracts for wind generators, photovoltaics, biofuel processing plants and no doubt nuclear power stations, than about the multidimensional change which is the real need.

In fact 'big business' and therefore also government is sure to do its best to convince us that the last thing we need to do is to change our rampantly materialistic lifestyles. That, after all, might mean a diminution of the gross domestic product, a zero or two removed from the pay cheque of top executives and less controlling power over the electorate. Carry on with a bit of recycling and green energy by all means, but let us take care of the big picture, say industrial leaders and political affiliates.

At the heart of the multidimensional crisis in which we find ourselves, is a truly extraordinary phenomenon, which surpasses the surprises thrown up by nature's very predictable and increasingly violent fever. This is the degree of passivity, unawareness and general apathy displayed by a large segment of the world's well educated citizens when faced by the realisation that the very survival of the ship that carries us through the universe is now at stake. The alarm bell has been ringing for two or three decades, getting louder with each passing year; but, rather than responding to this wake-up call, many are only now rubbing their eyes and wondering what time it is? The bedclothes feel nice and warm, and it's still dark outside...

The real time is half an hour after midnight and the roots are trembling.

A great portion of humanity appears to be sleepwalking through life in a vacuous daze, unwilling to address the reality: that we are in a crisis largely of our own making and need to take urgent action to avert disaster. This state of general passivity cannot solely be explained by the addictive quality of a materialistic, money-obsessed society. Nor can it be put down solely to a lack of awareness, or even an apathetic disinterest in world affairs. Even some people's total reliance on 'the experts' to put things right with some new technical fix, hardly answers the question why so many people's instincts should be so unresponsive to the cries of nature and to the cries of fellow human beings. None of these suppositions explain the extraordinary levels of detached 'disinterest' in the unravelling crisis going on around us all. A large segment of mankind appears to be suffering from a malaise which echoes the geophysical and psychic malaise of our planet.

The laws of nature and the laws of man appear to have become separated from one another. They have gone off at a tangent, and at a steadily accelerating speed. Industrial man has, as we explore in other chapters, somehow anaesthetised and sanitised himself from the underlying pulse of life, and in so doing now often sees positive life forces as more threatening than helpful.

Certain segments of society, with strong vested interests, have successfully utilised their powers of persuasion to lure large numbers of citizens into uncritically adopting a 'consumer' view of life. This equals: you can and should have anything and everything you want in this life - just find a way of earning the money to make it happen!

This drive to consume is a relatively recent phenomenon, even in terms of man's recent history, and in the past applied only to a relatively small segment of society. Now consumerism – 'shopping' is a national and international obsession on a very large scale. Hypermarkets, and vast shopping malls, would never have exploded onto our fields and town centres if their owners had not been confident of filling the aisles with thousands upon thousands of avid credit card waving customers.

In the post-industrial societies of North America and northern Europe, and now increasingly in other fast growing economies, the wheels of 'economic progress' are dependent upon maintaining the upward momentum of this crazed consumer boom. Nothing, in effect, is more important than keeping people buying. In this perverse materialistic stampede, it matters not what is being bought, only how much wealth the system is generating.

Only a financial crash of the dimensions that we are now witnessing appears capable of puncturing the obsession with materialistic growth.

In order to ensure that the consumer-driven status quo is maintained, those at the receiving end of the generated wealth will go to extreme lengths to ensure their power is not undermined or threatened. It is strategically so important for the vast transnational corporations to retain their hold over society, that they have devised highly sophisticated forms of propaganda, marketing and mind control to do so. These are directly targeted at the receptive antennae of the human brain, and often at the subliminal level. TV is particularly adept at this, but all areas of mainstream media are caught up in perpetuating the process of consumerist indoctrination.

Is it any wonder then, that people are sleepwalking through life and that our planet is groaning and suffering under the sheer weight of junk generated by this pathogenic shopping disease? Have you ever paused to reflect on the sheer volume of concrete and tarmac that continues to be laid on the earth's surface just to keep the ever-larger and more numerous CO_2 spouting articulated lorries moving from one place to another?

Traversing the world with their cargoes of largely useless consumables?

The ever greater number of runways needed to shift ever greater numbers of bargain-hunting holidaymakers around the exotic beauty spots and shopping havens of the world?

The thousands of new aircraft that are being built to keep this great buzz going? The millions of tonnes of carbon rich kerosene dumped in the already suffocating atmosphere? And what about the sterile cling film wrapped foods that fill the plastic shelves of the ever expanding supermarket chains, whose combined UK refrigerated power consumption requires an entire nuclear power plant's electricity generation to maintain it?

Then consider the fertility of the land from which this food comes. It is now so depleted of natural vitality by years of monocultural, agro-chemical assisted mass production that only extra strong doses of synthetic nitrogen and accompanying herbicides, fungicides and pesticides can ensure that anything grows on it at all. The list is endless; I don't need to go on. There are already hundreds of books exposing this merciless greed in great detail, and showing what unprecedented levels of destruction it is having on life on earth. However, the situation continues to deteriorate, in spite of all the warnings and all the knowledge that we now possess concerning the destruction which is being perpetrated upon our bruised and battered planet.

Once we realise what we are doing, that we are engaged in an act of premeditated murder affecting all species and all nations, then the fire of change must be ignited within us. If it is not, we are only fit for consignment to the severely overfilled rubbish pits that are the repository of our selfish extravagance.

As the situation continues to deteriorate, so do solutions begin to emerge. It's something of a race against time, but interestingly, it is not a race that will be won by rushing more by a carefully judged use of common sense. The challenge to redesign daily life so that waste and pollution becomes all but eliminated is attracting some very creative and talented individuals.

An understanding is emerging that all waste matter can be transformed, transferred and even reutilised, at a cost. The trouble is that, in most cases, the cost is too high. So far, the amount of finite energy going into the waste recycling and transformation process is still too great to balance out the energy/cost equation. So clearly the conclusion we must reach is that it is best to produce no waste at all. *Transitioning towards this goal is a fundamental requirement of the consumer society.*

The beginning of the change towards a 'no waste' society starts with a change of attitude in ourselves. A diminishing of the urge 'to have' and a nourishing of the urge 'to be'. A movement from largely material obsessions, to more self motivated *aspirations*. So fundamental is 'energy' to our lives, that we should question every aspect of its use at all moments. So we might just as well start by recognising that the first and foremost waste of all energy (human and generated) is *wrong thinking*. This is where the garbage begins! Change our 'wrong thinking' into 'right thinking' and we have the launch pad for 'right-doing'. And 'right-doing' is the true foundation for human and planetary longevity.

How do we know what is 'right-doing'?

It is best, when first approaching the subject of what is – and what is not– 'wrong thinking', to draw a clean slate, and start again from here. So from the moment of waking, and repeatedly throughout the day, try asking this question: am I using my human energy positively or negatively? And am I encouraging others to use their energies positively? Whenever I am not using my energy *positively*, I seem to be further contributing to the problem: the waste tip. My negative energy and the cynical 'it's not my concern' thinking process, is the same as my discarded rubbish. All it does is to clog up the vibratory channels and bring me and others down...

Maybe it's true ... that if I fail to overcome my worst habits in this life, I will eventually be recycled and as part of the ever turning, great cyclic wheel of life, decay, death and return? Wow! If so, I may have to come back for another attempt to finally get it right . . . *but do I want to come back again, only to find even more garbage, including the junk that I left behind thinking it didn't matter?* More garbage, more negativity and more misery? NO THANKS! So I conclude ... I really have no choice, but to start now the process of clearing up the inner and outer mess, and engaging in positive change.. no matter how small the initial steps may be. Hmm ... as my confidence rises and the momentum builds, I'll be able to take on more and more responsibility ... for myself ... my neighbourhood ... and even my planet! Yes!

6. Energy and Time

The amount of outside energy we seek to utilise in our daily lives is proportionate to the levels of inner energy that remain unrealised in us. Our capacity to achieve the extraordinary is innate. It is innate in every baby born into our world, and, as we explore in the chapter on education, it is largely our mismanagement of the process we call 'education' that holds back a revolution in our evolution as human beings.

As suggested in the previous chapter, the first and foremost waste of energy is wrong thinking. Millions of megajoules of human energy are wasted every day by negative and generally misdirected and useless thoughts that crowd the human brain and clog the communication networks: put an end to this 'thought garbage' and we will already be making a major energy saving contribution to our planet and far beyond it.

Only once we are well-accustomed to thinking positively –and laterally– about the majority of problems that confront us, can we even begin to work out a desirable 'energy plan' for the nation, let alone the world.

In almost all youngsters and adolescents, a constantly bubbling energy is literally popping most of the time. In fact, a lot of adult energy is spent trying to contain it within civilised norms, quite often unsuccessfully! But a wonderful and beautiful source of energy is there nonetheless.

Some go into adult life still exuding and guiding their energies into whatever appropriate channels they can create or find, but a great many more drift into more settled and secure routines that dissipate creative energies, bleeding away the bright element of genius. Society suffers accordingly – and deeply.

Therefore, one should start by asking this fundamental question: "how should we apply 'energy' during our terrestrial existence?" This question enquires about both the metaphysical and earthbound purpose of 'energy'. It presumes an open book of human and cosmic potentiality, rather than a more cautious preordained view of life's supposed limitations. Life, in the fullest sense of the word, has no limitations.

So, in the current debate on how better to utilise generated terrestrial energy supplies to combat global warming and other environmentally destructive excesses, it is imperative to reconsider much more than just questions of how to better insulate our homes, cut back on fossil fuels and redesign motorcars, power stations and refrigerators, to give very low CO_2 emissions. While such steps have a certain merit (in their own right) we need to take a much more radical step if we are to bring about lasting change for the better.

Such a step, or more likely 'leap', *involves reassessing the whole energy equation in the light of a clear vision of a very different future from the one our politicians or utility companies have in mind for us.* One in which our energies are directed into bold, life affirmative actions, and not just the day in day out demands of the working week.

This implies being open to finding increasing time in order to tune into metaphysical energy flows, that, once we have opened our receptors to their mysterious powers, unveil to us what steps can be taken to move us onto other –and higher– planes of awareness and richer fields of experience.

It is a question of learning to recognise and respond to the directives of our inner signposts, and to the voice of our deeper conscience. Practising disciplines that help us down this road will enable us to move away from the habit of unashamedly using our relentless will power to get what we want out of life. A habit that, in the end, ends up taking us further and further away from our deeper instincts and true life callings.

By relaxing the hold that our mundane will-power retains over us, we can start to grow into a new feeling of being 'connected up' with greater positive life forces, and becoming increasingly imbued with a desire to get actively involved in promoting all that advances their cause – rather than just our own!

So, if I am correct in asserting that the amount of outside 'processed' energy that we seek to utilise in our daily lives is broadly proportionate to the amount of inner energy that remains unrealised in us, *we can only solve our earth's precipitous ecological dilemma by realigning our human energies with the unseen universal forces that guide us towards making the right choices in life.*

Although this might sound somewhat abstract, it is not. There are many tried and tested techniques for helping us to tunein to universal energies, and there are thousands of aspirants already drawing benefit from adopting one or other of these techniques. All true attempts to create an enduring and positive equilibrium in life require a continual process of nurturing and counterbalancing our God given practical, spiritual, social and artistic drives. *It is towards making this process the hub around which everything else evolves, that our main energies should be aligned, society directed and education systems committed. Only in this way can the symptoms of global destruction be genuinely addressed and transformed.*

Digging the soil, planting seeds and harvesting the resulting crop, when performed light heartedly –and with the companionship of others– need be no less a creative experience than performing in a work of dramatic art, playing in an orchestra or painting a fine picture. However, we have categorised such skills to appear to be at almost opposite ends of the spectrum. Our professions, skills and talents have been divided into false, stereotyped compartments; consequently, our minds struggle to try and grasp the underlying connectivity that exists between all of them, between all the necessities of life.

Need the construction of a well-designed human or farm animal shelter be any less of an artistic pursuit than creating the stage set for a work of dramatic art? Need the turning over and nurturing of the soil be any less of a creative expression than the act of carving a piece of sculpture? Need the knitting of a lambswool sweater be any less of a creative act than applying coloured oils to a newly stretched canvas? Provided the motive for all these actions is pure and the energies are fundamentally united, there is no sense in stigmatising them to suit the perverse fashions of human snobbery. It is only our distorted observations that divide them against each other, draining out the dynamic life juices that comprise our shared universal energy.

So, before going along with the widely disseminated assumption that we need to generate as much, if not more energy to everlastingly fuel the 'growth' of our bloated consumer economies –stop to consider if this supposedly sacrosanct economic principle is really a desirable– or a self destructive– plan for the world's future?

So many hundreds of wind farms, so many millions of solar panels, or so many nuclear power stations – just to be able to further indulge in our current energy addiction? Stop for a minute, and ask yourself the following questions: do we really want to go to the trouble of generating energy –even 'green energy'– simply in order to maintain the same wasteful routines that currently preoccupy consumer fixated societies around the world? Is there no more fulfilling use to be made of our energies during this life time? Is shopping really the best thing since Beethoven?

My guess is, that if we were 50% more creatively fulfilled (and realised) in our daily lives, we would need (and use) 50% less technologically processed energy. We should be designing the future with this in mind – setting our ultimate target on a 100% 'self-realisation' target. At that point, no external processed energy will be required at all.

7. Time and Energy

Time is another of our relatively recent inventions. Time is useful in dividing absolute energy flows into abstract segments, used largely to justify financial considerations or defined work schedules. It has been both a blessing and a curse; but rather more the latter.

The celestial movement of heavenly bodies combined with the waxing and waning moon, and the sun's twenty four hour cycle of appearance and disappearance over the eastern and western horizons, already provide the basis for a certain broad delineation of time. For the purpose of establishing a rhythm for human activity, the circadian movement of nature is probably our best guide.

However, its further dissection into hours, minutes and seconds has served the functioning of commercial life and the efficiency of largely mundane activities, far more than it has enabled us to gain a greater comprehension of our universality. Consequently, we tend to operate like clockwork when we could be operating like a free flowing work of art.

In essence, time does not exist. However, change does. Everything 'of this world' is changing all the time. Every cell, chromosome and nucleus in our bodies is either dying or being born –at all times. Every tree is growing, decaying and being reborn again from fallen seed– at all times.

Only the invisible flame of life remains constant; that which stands behind –and empowers– all temporal change. A flame which is imperceptible to the human eye and not easily assimilated by our rational thought process.

We have developed a bad association with the word 'change', because so much worldly change is based on actions that are superficial and largely destructive to life; whereas the deeper, nature driven rhythms of change are the carriers and expressions of universal harmony: we are happier immediately we get in tune with these underlying energy flows.

It is very easy to become victimised by our man made time. We all struggle to find a way of resolving the rhythms of nature with the self-imposed demands of the time dictated working day. In attempting to do this, and by placing some sort of financial value on the passage of time, we have put the human being under a lot of unnecessary physical and mental stress. We have made our order and rhythm of life more important than the universal rhythms that regulate nature, and in the process we have forgotten that we are part of that nature.

The more complex our daily divisions of time, the more fragmented are our lives. The more fragmented our lives, the more desperate do we become to fit all the things we wish to achieve into the times allocated for them, and the faster we run (or drive) in order to try and keep up with our constantly slipping self-imposed timetables. Heeellp!

Is this the best use we can make of our time here on planet earth? Dividing up our days in order to organise more efficiently our already overstretched, unsustainable and unrewarding lifestyles? Everybody needs to earn money, but when the process overlays our sensitivities and deeper needs with a thousand abstractions and distractions, it is surely time to call a halt – and try and work out another way forward.

All these self-imposed fractional time divisions lead us into making the wrong use of time, energy and money. Relentless adhesion to such schematic divisions leads us to becoming net contributors to a broader state of global imbalance and stress; leading in turn, to an utterly wasteful use of both human nervous energy and the terrestrial 'mined energy' required to keep it all going. The net result is translated into ever-building levels of abstraction – and general fatigue to mind, body and spirit. Although hard to avoid, all 'rushing' has a knock-on effect further contributing to the already over-frenetic pace of life. Time appears to move faster, and we seem to have less and less of it.

We should try to stop distractedly rushing around, and instead learn how to slow down, calm and centre ourselves: to "Be Here Now". Thus bringing 'time' to us rather than us always chasing time. In this calmed state of 'being', terrestrial time fades away, and only the state of "I am Here Now" prevails. The 'I am' being an impersonal and metaphysical state as opposed to an egocentric and personal one. A recognition that at our centre we are universal cosmic beings (not just bread winners) deeply connected in a loving relationship with our Creator.

We can slow ourselves down, and in so doing, gain a new sense of self-control. For instance, by taking even 15 minutes in each day to sit quietly, allowing oneself to "Be"– conjoined calmly with nature and the cosmos, and removed from earthly distractions.

Controlled deep breathing, in conjunction with regular yoga exercises – known in India as 'Asanas' – is a fine way of reining-in our often turbulent minds and emotions, and gaining a fresh perspective on what may appear to be unresolveable problems.

The end objective is to set in motion a whole other way of living our lives; one which transforms linear time and energy, and enables us to find lasting and deeply satisfying levels of fulfilment, coupled with a refreshed sense of direction...

Having got a taste for this, we can go on to explore the rich library of writings and teachings that exist in all cultures and faiths that guide and encourage us to experience a greater and more all encompassing sense of love and compassion for everything around us – ourselves included. We can start treating ourselves as Human Beings.

A major part of 'taking control of our outer lives' involves 'taking control of our inner lives': awakening that calm, centred place of inner balance. Starting again from "Here" gives us a wholly other perspective on the razzmatazz of our restless society. A perspective that makes us aware that we *can start directing our destiny, rather than allowing circumstances to direct us.* Once we are again – or for the first time – in touch with our deeper selves, we can tune into the subtle, intuitional guidance, that enables us to tackle more confidently the innumerable tasks to be undertaken to heal our planet and re-energise our local communities. In this way, earthly time is transformed, and each day takes on a fresh sense of purpose and significance.

The process of confronting, head on, each road block and hurdle on this journey, and determinedly setting about overcoming them and affecting positive change, brings a constantly renewing source of energy with it. The friction involved in making the effort taps new resources in us.

This is a very different energy from the one we plug into to satisfy our habitual material cravings. It is a self-generated dynamic energy, wholly different in constitution from that which leads us to lean on technically generated outside energy sources for our ease and comforts. It is a transforming process, having the power to heal, rejuvenate and inspire, leading us to discover new and exciting dimensions beyond the repetitive two and three dimensional worlds which most of us take for reality.

The process of 'grasping the nettle' or 'taking the bull by the horns' is actually our best means of gaining such inner strength and cosmic support. There is no substitute for taking action (inner and outer) – of deliberately setting forth to transform heavy, negative energies into light positive joys.

This process can be aided by allowing the warrior spark in ourselves to be ignited and not being afraid to join others who have already set forth to take 'direct action' to right the wrongs that otherwise distress and repress us. *Only when we feel a sense of inner empowerment can we gain a true insight into what degrees of outside, technically generated power we really need to sustain ourselves.*

In the interim, the best we can do is to act responsibly, cease wasting energy and support all efforts to cut back on obviously polluting activities. In other words, cultivate common sense.

8. Man and Animal

The relationship animal/man is a powerful one. Physiologically it is recognised that there is only a tiny difference in the DNA of the higher mammalian species (i.e. apes) and that of man. The fact is that we are animals, and animals can rightly be ascribed many of the attributes of man. For thousands of years we have existed together, sharing our food and terrain, and during this time a great bond has developed a certain mutual affinity and respect.

We know how loving animals can be and how curative and calming is this love they so freely give. This is particularly evident in dogs, but is also true of horses, cows, pigs, cats, and all sorts of other beasts of the field and birds of the air. All these creatures also have powerful survival instincts, and will fight to the death for their existence if necessary.

The domesticated farm animal has contributed untold support to the human race over the millennia. Both as a source of meat, milk and clothing, and as a beast of labour. To this day there are millions of donkeys, horses, cows, buffaloes and oxen helping man to till his fields and sow his corn. It has been so since biblical times and long before.

One of the first processed foods consumed by man was a curd cheese, which formed itself by chance, when a donkey carrying a small sack of milk across rough terrain produced just the right amount of swaying movement to cause the milk to coagulate into a basic form of cheese. This event is purported to have happened in Anatolia (Turkey) some three to four thousand years before Christ.

Farm animals also fertilise the land. Many poor soils have been brought to life by the diligent use of farmyard manures, and as ruminant's dung added to the compost heap. The use of cow dung in building and insulating houses and huts is still widely practised in the more pastoral areas of the world, and claims of its efficiency as an insulator are widespread. Under certain specific conditions it also has unusual healing qualities; these are recognised and applied by Ayurvedic practitioners, under an ancient practice known as 'Homa Therapy'.

There are too many positive attributes to name when it comes to describing the richness that our animal cousins bring into the world.

However, a great tragedy has arisen in our shared relationship with domesticated farm animals, and a terrible injustice has been perpetrated, by consigning certain animals to fill the role of factory farm inputs and outputs, their short lives being witnessed only by the person who feeds them and the person who kills them. Or in both cases, the man who presses the buttons on the machines that dispense their antibiotic-laden, genetically modified food and the conveyor belt killing machine that dispatches them.

Let us not call such individuals farmers. Anyone who can endure such work is more suited to working in a morgue. So soulless, perverse and debased is this system of food production, that it defies words to adequately describe the levels of insentient and callous inhumanity to which we have descended in order to have invented such animal concentration camps. At the other end of this chain, Mr and Mrs X, walking into their favourite neon-lit, sanitised supermarket, will encounter their animal cousin as an apparently nice piece of tender chicken or pork, hygienically wrapped in cling film, and presented in a little polystyrene tray: a 'special offer', the supermarket bargain of the day. As Mr and Mrs X observe their evening meal, they are particularly interested in the price. Hmm, is there not an even cheaper broiler at another supermarket down the road?

Yes, there will always be a cheaper broiler somewhere, so long as man regards the bird as nothing more than a cheap piece of edible flesh. So long as we close ourselves off from ourselves, and from our relationship with all sentient life forms that are part and parcel of our living world. So long as we don't ask any difficult questions regarding the buying policy of our favourite chain store.

Factory farms are the places where thousands of animals, usually pigs and chickens, are kept in vast airless, sunless sheds, with only the very minimum space in which to move. The pigs on concrete cubicles and the hens in metal cages. They live under strip lighting, kept on 18 or 24 hours a day to encourage constant eating for weight gain and continuous egg laying. Their diet typically consists of finely ground soya beans and maize, with added prophylactic doses of antibiotics to stave off the risk of disease that such environments always attract. The antibiotics also act as a growth promoter, causing faster weight gain. The maize and soya used in most European and North American factory farm units, is genetically modified, and produced on vast monocultural prairies whose soils have been rendered so sterile and lifeless, that only agrichemically assisted plants can grow on them.

The pigs and broiler hens have frighteningly short lives – if indeed you can call their time on earth 'life'. The broilers (hens reared for meat) may make 2 months before slaughter, the pigs around three and a half months. The laying hens are as useful as their laying ability, which is encouraged by a diet of high protein soya, with added medication to keep them from being struck down with disease. Into this feed are added special synthetic colours to make the yolks turn an appealing orange colour. If these colours were not added, the yolks would be pale grey, and no one would eat them. The typical life span of these birds is three months.

I have kept free range hens on my farm. Their homes are movable wooden houses, with fifty hens in each house, poles to perch on, and constant day-time access to green grass fields. Their diet of cracked wheat and whatever they forage off the land enables them to continue steady but un-spectacular egg production for three to four years. Their pale orange yolks are formed by the green matter they eat as part of their natural outdoor foraging.

I have also kept outdoor, free range pigs. They root around in the earth with their snouts, and wander content-edly where they will within the confines of the field and also sometimes the neighbour's! They can live this way for many years, the sows producing many litters of healthy piglets. The extra food they receive being a blend of home produced cereals and vegetable wastes.

There are many farms that rear their animals on systems approximately halfway between the two described here; trying to find a balance between earning a reasonable re-turn on their investment, while managing to keep up good standards of animal welfare. These are not factory farms, just sensibly run family farming enterprises, whose financial survival is under intense pressure because the mass produc-tion factory farms undercut the market for their produce.

But it is the supermarkets that call the tune. They dem-and large quantities of uniform eggs and meat, regularly supplied and at precise dates. They like to deal with a few very large suppliers. Suppliers that keep 30,000 hens in one vast daylight-less shed or 3,000 pigs in similarly confined conditions. The supermarkets are ruthless in their determ-ination to get their products very cheap, so Mr and Mrs X can get their 'bargain'. The only way the producer can meet the rock bottom prices on offer, is by finding ways of raising their animals –and lots of them– at equally rock bottom costs.

Mass production factory farming has, up till now, been presented as the only way the producer can make a profit based on the unacceptably low price or offer for the end product. So Mr and Mrs X –and all other thoughtless consumers– it is you who are giving the supermarkets the perfect excuse to encourage the animal rearing methods of the factory farms, rather than the methods utilised by organic and good traditional farmers. Your insistent demand for impossibly cheap meat and the 'special bargain' drives the factory farm conveyor belt, and gives credibility to systems that have no credibility in terms of human and animal dignity. I have not mentioned milk production. It would take another book to tell the whole story and others have done this already.

Animal and man can, and should, serve each other. But we have an absolute responsibility to cease mercilessly exploiting our cousins for our own greed and short-sighted self-satisfaction. Once aware of the plight of such mass produced sentient birds and animals, it amounts to a criminal act to insist on continuing to purchase them. If one is buying on price – because no other meat seems affordable, it is better to eat such food much less frequently, and then try to source humanely reared, better quality meat.

There is nothing more rewarding than to raise animals and crops to a quality, standard and price that gives satisfaction to all concerned. Farmers are stewards of the land and also its trustees. Their role puts them in the position of being guardians of the quality of life in all aspects of their farms, but outstandingly so for the animals in their care, whom they come to see as a sort of extended family.

For a good farmer, these animals' health and welfare always takes precedence over financial considerations. His or her pride and humanity is at stake around the clock; and tragically, many a farmer would rather take his or her own life than see their farm fall into disrepute or insolvency. The latter leads to anonymous ownership by the bank from whom the farmers borrowed the investment money to set up a working business.

Between themselves, many farmers talk of making money and of the productive qualities of their animals and soils. But privately, most nurture soft hearts and a great love of the way of life, however tough.

We live in a time of unprecedented disconnection between town and country, and of deep misunderstanding and ignorance. This has enabled corporations, greedy for profit, to exploit the resulting lack of discernment amongst a large body of consumers. The wound this has caused is deep, and our farm animals have been especially vulnerable. But now is the time to heal these wounds. *Now* is always the best time to mend things, and newly acquired awareness must be followed by action to bring about positive change. The formula for this change lies in kindling some warmth in our hearts, then listening to – and acting on – the voice of our conscience.

Animal and man/ man and animal, travel together on the path of life. We are travelling companions. But we humans have the power to organise our domesticated animals for our own ends. So if our own ends are broadly compassionate, we will give them as good a life as we are able, and they will reward us equally. This is the path of non exploitation and balanced relationship. If we participate knowingly in utilising our consumer power to support animal concentration camps, we ultimately kill both the animal and the human in ourselves.

9. Art, Education and Spirit: United

"We cannot solve our present problems using the same type of thinking which created them." Albert Einstein

Being artistic is not the opposite of being practical. Far from it: to be a true artist one must draw on practical skills. Likewise to be truly practical, one must draw on creative skills. However, due to the advent of mass production of goods and specialisation of skills, these two facets of humankind's potentiality have been separated out over time and made to appear as opposing qualities.

Those who channel their artistic skills into making fine foods, forged metals, agricultural equipment, pottery bowls and handsome wooden tables were –and still are– called 'artisans'. Here we see the direct link between art and practical necessity. The two are united. The artisan is an individual concerned with quality in all things he or she does. Quality of this nature cannot be mass produced on a factory production line for an ever increasing monetary return – although it can be imitated in this way.

Everyone born into this world is an artist in potentiality. Every baby born is, in his or her innocence, a fertile seed of art and spirit. An as yet unexpressed aspirant, deeply curious about the make-up of life, reaching out to experience and touch the cosmic game which is 'cause' and 'effect', and express wonderment at the way even the smallest objects move and resonate.

A society that wishes to find fulfilment will need to take note of this precious seed, and ensure that it is carefully planted in a fertile soil. The word education comes from the Latin 'educare', meaning 'to lead out from'. *So 'education' is the process whereby those who take on the role of educators (teachers) have the task of encouraging that which is already there in potential, to become realised in actuality.*

Teachers take many forms: mothers and fathers, older brothers and sisters, elders, leaders, craftsmen, school/university teachers, to name but a few. But there is one crucial qualification: to be a good teacher one must share with the child that curiosity which acts as a spur to and impetus for – creativity in all daily concerns. Without this curiosity there can be no positive process of change. No positive change, means being stuck in a downward spiral of stagnation, decay and ultimately death. This is largely the situation we find ourselves in today.

How has it got so bad?

An overemphasis on academic achievement has dominated western educational programmes for many decades, increasingly at the expense of vocational skills. Such an overemphasis on academic and intellectual strengths creates an imbalance in overall emotional development, starving children and young adults of the all-round development of their potentialities which brings balance and harmony into everyday life.

Strong institutional pressures to turn out stereotyped individuals, whose main purpose is to maintain the vested interests of society, have remained largely unchallenged throughout academic and western school systems. Some notable exceptions have demonstrated more holistic approaches, but such approaches were not adopted by mainstream educational establishments, which have continued to use the old formula to this day.

Within this system, even those teachers with the best intentions, struggle to elicit and nurse creativity and curiosity in their pupils and students.

When we consider what factors underlie the deep unease and restless nature of our western societies, we cannot help but note the role of education as making a dominant contribution. What we call education today has little to do with encouraging real creativity, or indeed, life curiosity. Rather than being an attempt to 'lead out from' and to realise the latent potential in each child or young person, contemporary education systems (and most earlier ones) are more concerned with attempts to 'push into'. To ensure heads are crammed full of facts and figures and the knowledge required to pass the all important exams that ensure the school's place in today's highly competitive league tables. Also, of course, ensuring that students reach a higher level of education and a better chance of finding a job that will offer a good monetary return.

As long as education is primarily an exam factory, concerned with encouraging the young to conform to fixed patterns of learning, it will be impossible to change society for the better, and the current status quo will retain its sterile grip on all areas of our lives.

The fact that this is the situation we find ourselves in today, explains to a significant degree, why our societies are not evolving in a positive direction and becoming more generally enlightened. It also explains why neither we (nor our societies) are being positively shaped by the real potential which remains innate and largely untapped in nearly all of us.

Although words such as 'progress' are blithely used to describe the stumbling advances of a largely technologically fixated society, it is – upon examination – often a deeply misleading concept. 'Progress' which goes hand in hand with, or is dependent upon, the misuse and abuse of irreplaceable natural resources – including human life cannot be seen as anything other than a deliberate deception. A twisting of language to convey a sense of improvement, while in reality things are steadily getting worse.

Unless and until artistry and spirit, in contact with nature and formative practical skills, form the centre ground in society, this regressive state will continue and both human and planetary life will be suffocated.

When the great creative potential that exists in every individual cannot find positive outward expression, it turns inward, and becomes a destructive force. Our societies are littered with such examples. It is education's role to ensure this does not happen, that the spirit is led out from its inner sanctum and is channelled into the creative shaping and moulding of a civil society which is always getting better, always evolving into a more subtle and more meaningful expression of love, beauty and joy. This is the only true meaning of 'Progress'.

Spiritual human development is equally neglected. At school level, it is typically consigned to some classes in religious belief systems, including (at best) those embracing a number of different faiths and diverse cultural backgrounds.

However, spirit is not solely to be found in religious writings or the practices of the church. *It is more true to say that churches have claimed ownership of spiritual knowledge and the right to teach it.* Prior to the pre-eminence of Judaeo-Christian teachings in western societies, there existed more informal and diversified ways of engendering spiritual aspiration and of passing spiritual knowledge.

So-called pagan rituals and festivities directly linked Spirit and the Land, harnessing energies of nature and offering them back to the Creator in ritualised and seasonal expressions of joy and thanks for the bounty of nature and the safely collected harvest.

On such occasions, the whole community came together, finding spontaneous and energetic expressions of emotional outflowing that released tensions and stimulated the senses. Such expressions are spiritual in nature, that is to say, inherently spiritual. They express the spirit of man in recognition of his dependence upon, and interdependence with, nature and the source of all life.

Later, the joyous movements and dramatic gestures and sounds that burst out on these occasions, became separated from each other. They became separate disciplines within what we call the 'arts': dance, theatre, painting, music and poetry. They also became uprooted from their original countryside settings, developing in cities of culture as 'fine arts'.

This not only rendered the ritual element obsolete, but also confined the genuine ecstasy of the original experience, to a pseudo halfway house and often faked imitation.

Much of what we call entertainment today is nothing more than an irreverent and unseemly jumble of such pseudo-art. Television stations pump out such entertainment in evermore glitzy extravaganzas. They are received in the living rooms of the world by individuals slumped on spongy sofas, their minds dulled and dumbed by the reckless and directionless rush of the all-consuming consumer society. It is a thoroughly debilitating cocktail, which only succeeds in taking us further and further away from our real selves.

Ritual is an important tool in bringing us back to our real selves. A powerful tool for bringing discipline and order into our deeper lives. The rituals associated with church ceremonies are often sought out at times of personal difficulty or tragedy – and they have their place. However they seldom take one further than a fulfilment of the need of the moment: the need for solace and prayer.

What is needed is a deeper awakening of the different stages of development of body, mind and spirit. An evolutionary adventure with a definite end goal: the full realisation of our extraordinary, but as yet latent potentials.

This 'initiation' must, by its nature, be a process where the experience of pain, loneliness and insecurity are *allowed to be fully experienced* – as a prelude to deeper and more meaningful experiences in the future.

We need to recognise that such experiences are an essential part of growing up. Their suppression puts a brake on the natural maturity of the individual and leads to a sense of feeling stuck in between two worlds; neither here nor there. Neither a child nor an adult – in the full meaning of those states.

Rituals and initiations have long been recognised and practised as important ways of guiding us through such processes of change, including the basic biological changes that take place at different points in our overall growing process. They are about ensuring that we do indeed *go right through* the necessary transforming process and emerge out at the other end – as new beings. Most importantly, not leaving individuals feeling inhibited, helpless and frightened when facing such a fundamental process of nature at work.

In order to make some real progress in this field, it is absolutely essential for all avenues of society to accept and acknowledge the need for this *deep* process of change. Acknowledge it as a state we need to go through, in order to become more profoundly self-expressed.

The process of what is nowadays often labelled a state of 'mental sickness', can, upon examination, often be found to be part of a necessary process of change. A process that has to be undergone in order for the individual to reach deeper levels of self-awareness and awareness of others. When society itself is operating on the borders of clinical insanity, what is called 'mental sickness' can actually be a reactive process to this greater sickness ultimately expressed as the road to a cure. A process of purging and burning off (or dissolving) mental obstructions, to reveal the positive emotions that lie buried underneath.

It is convenient for leaders of a dying, materialistically conformist society, to label such a process of awakening as 'an illness'; but this is just a way of camouflaging the fact that *the real sickness is embedded in an implacable devotion to the worn out dogmas of a deeply impaired status quo.*

Education, in order to fulfil its deeper meaning, will have to incorporate a real sense of compassion and understanding for the deep process of change we human beings need to go through in the course of our development. We must re-find proper ways of supporting each other on this journey – not turn away out of fear or ignorance.

Art, Education and Spirit now have to be reunited, as an imperative for the rejuvenation of humanity. Not in a romantic attempt to recreate a past era that never really existed except in some sporadic moments – but to do something which the human soul has been longing for since the beginning of our planetary existence. This process of reunification will form part of an agrarian revolution, because that is the stage for the re-emergence of new life. Man cannot go on indefinitely separated from nature and participation in the process that secures his sustenance. The urban energies that contributed to the evolution of modern society (both good and bad) are now largely a spent force. They are unsustainable, abstracted and uncommunicative to the deeper spirit of man.

There is no set formula for reinspiring a sense of purpose in life, but the following guidelines should be observed:

Starting at the local community/parish level: primary schools can encourage children to become aware of the subtlety of nature; the changing colours of leaves at times of seasonal change; the feeling of damp soil in the hands; the sound of the wind; the colour of the sky; the shapes formed by clouds and the different cadences of birdsong.

Then the act of planting some seeds in the soil and observing their growth into plants, leading to the experience of picking berries and fruits – tasting the edible ones and comparing their flavours. Articulating the differences in taste and the textures of these fruits.

At a slightly later age, pupils should have a chance to help out on local working farms, gathering harvests, feeding and tending to livestock and learning how to make butter, cheese and other simple foods. One of this is extra-curricular activity, it must be absolutely central to the main curriculum. That which is crucial to everyday survival should also be most important in schools; it is as simple as that.

Schools should have their own small plot of land on which to carry forward this process. If this is not possible, then local allotments or a neighbouring friendly farm can suffice. Using our hands for purposeful work is a vital experience – it stimulates blood circulation and feeds the brain with positive perceptive and intuitive energies.

Skills that are essential to our later life are always best acquired young. Knowing how to grow food is the most basic, elemental skill of all. Building and construction skills follow on, as does learning the art of craftsmanship in all its diversity. This is best achieved on a one to one basis with skilled individual craftsmen and women, and not necessarily in the confines of the school building.

An aesthetic feel for design, scale and proportion must also be encouraged during school years, as should a sensitive appreciation of colour and texture. Nature will always be the best teacher of this. The stark primary colours of toys and games that are in favour today are not conducive to an appreciation of subtlety, and should consequently be discouraged.

Artistic courses should interlink with essential basic academic studies throughout the learning process. Drama is a powerful medium for bringing out the creative spirit in young people. It has the potential to positively harness energies that otherwise can run amok. It can also help young-sters to overcome inhibitions that otherwise may remain a block on their life development[5]. Music has magical prop-erties as well: learning to master a musical instrument has been shown to stimulate many other aspects of learning and give a positive push to academic achievement. Poetry and story telling also deserve a special place in the curriculum. Poetry challenges individuals to form word pictures, and to develop rhythms that have profound significance in the expression of inner feelings and subtle foresight. Photogra-phy, film and craft skills should have expression within the school curriculum.

Learning to harness creative expression is not a nicety to be relegated to after hours activities or occasional lessons. It is, as has been said earlier, at the essence of our ability to acquire sensibility and bring proper motivation into a world that is in desperate need of such input. *When educational pro-grammes are planned, they should be centred around the need to stimulate positive change in society as a whole and to take further that which is already proved to be good.*

At primary and secondary school age, sports and phys-ical activities that encourage good physical coordination are recommended, but so too is the furthering of practical skills already alluded to at the primary school level. At all points of development, a holistic programme is essential. Pupils should be challenged to write incisive essays, to read thought-provoking literature, to grapple with the laws of physics and maths and to explore deep spiritual thinking. Already, perceptions and ideas for ways radically to im-prove upon our current treatment of the planet – and each other – should emerge in young children and teenagers, and should be debated in special forums.

---

5 Working with small groups of children in the 1970s at the Institute for Crea-tive Development in Antwerp, Belgium, excellent results were achieved when a blance of academic and artistic studies were incorporated in the curriculum.

At the university level, one is supposed to be teaching and learning 'universality'. That which is 'of the universe': universal knowledge. This sort of knowledge is best experienced at a point in life when one has already acquired some life experience. So, either schools have to integrate life experience into the curriculum, or universities have to open their knowledge wealth to older life explorers, who have found out which of their talents they wish to deepen and develop.

Education is a constantly moving force. We are all students of life, all our lives. When the young see the old still seeking, they are at once attracted and wish to join the adventure; thus all are moving forward together on different planes of maturity – in one great flow of exploring, absorbing and celebrating life's secrets.

Our formal educational process, in its goal of bringing well-rounded, confident and life-hungry youngsters into the wider world, needs to respect the fundamental truth of this deep and enriching process, ensuring that it becomes the foundation of all that follows.

Communication and aspiration – as an art form

Real communication is an art form. Most of us do not communicate well. Nor are we good at listening. But when we are deeply moved by something, our communicative expression suddenly has extra resonance. In fact, it carries an emotional resonance which enters the listener at a different and more subtle frequency than the one which mundane conversation functions on. That is why, if we want to be effective communicators, we have to find ways of transmitting our deeper thoughts more directly and more honestly.

So if we are truly to understand one another, the art of communication needs to be cultivated and given great importance in society. We have allowed the power of words to be stolen from us, and have almost ceased caring, in the mundane rush to complete our daily tasks.

But space must be created, and time found, for real communication – and we must cease thinking that it doesn't matter if words like 'ocean' are removed from dictionaries and other elements of language are debased.

To understand each other we have to do something more than just hearing what each other is saying. *To understand* one another, involves opening our receptors at the emotional, spiritual and intuitive levels and then responding from these same levels. Only then can we start truly understanding and communicating with one another.

This in turn suggests that we need to channel our communicative energies in a more economical and thoughtful way; learn to recognise that 'chatter' is a form of waste, just like over-packaged foods. Indeed chattering aimlessly is a form of vocal pollution. This equally applies to radio, television and the written word. The 'media' should be standard setters for the art of communication, not polluters of it.

We are living in a time when the power of the word language is being neutralised and standardised to fit the corporate agenda, or shall we say 'consumer speak', thus squeezing out sentient word pictures and the beauty, wealth and resonance of the spoken and written word. George Orwell warned of such an event more than sixty years ago. Advertising, office jargon and the overrated value of 'commercial kudos' have combined to take language further and further from its roots, and render it less and less an expression of our deeper feelings.

The danger is all too apparent; if we corrupt our means of communication, we will ultimately fail to understand our own roots and cultural heritage, and we will also ultimately fail to understand ourselves. The word is a thing of beauty and sensuality; it is our primary tool of expression and description and it has been forged out of thousands of years of hard graft and tender nuance. We will discover a whole other form of poverty if we lose our immeasurably rich languages to some form of degraded, emotionless computer speak.

As with other pursuits, communication needs to refind expression at the community level and work back outwards. Just as artisan and agricultural skills are needed to craft our tools and grow our food, so too is good communication essential for conveying and sharing our hopes and aspirations. Losing meaningful words from our common discourse is the same as losing some indigenous plant from our terrestrial ecology; so we need to view our languages as 'rare breeds' and nurture them back into good health, just as we do with plants and animals. Here, poetry, drama, song, story telling and letter writing form an essential part of the process of conveying and communicating deeper feelings, deeper aspirations. Honing the art of communication is an everlasting process, and a constantly enriching one. It is an essential part of our expression as human beings.

Aspiration lies at the root of our urge to realise our potential, but it cannot find expression without an accompanying practical vision, plus a plan of action that will help to realise that vision. There is no substitute for taking action: once we aspire, taking action to fulfil our aspiration is the natural next step. Aspiration, without action, is like soil without a seed. In fact, if we passively leave the management of our society and our planet to others, we will not progress far down the path of our own hopes and ideals, and we will witness our aspirations shrivelling on the vine.

10. Youth Meets Wisdom

"We don't stop playing because we grow old, we grow old because we stop playing". George Bernard Shaw

When we are children, we also have a bit of adult in us – and when we are adults, we still retain an element of the child. We should rejoice in this fact, for it reveals the great continuity and repetition of the life cycle. In the acorn is the oak. On the oak is the acorn. There is no point when the child becomes purely an adult – and no longer a child, just as there is no point when the adult no longer carries the seed of childhood.

So why do we impose this artificial separation upon ourselves?

Why do we deny the reality? Perhaps because 'adulthood' has been identified as the time to give up one thing and to take on another: to conform to the role as bread winner, family raiser and career follower. Most businesses do not welcome the presence of childlike innocence, unless it can be bent to the task of making money. Most institutions demand loyalty to their particular credo, and the conformist behaviour pattern that gives this genre a certain image. Steady, unemotional, reasonably hard working, and politically correct. Thus, even if the school system has not stifled the child in us, the business world will soon finish the job.

We must revive the true relationship between child and adult, young and old, youth and wisdom. The best way to recognise the validity of this relationship is to observe a child's natural attraction to his or her grandmother or grandfather, and vice versa. The child sees a little of themselves in the elder, and the elder sees a little of themselves in the child. From this point, this foundation, we can rebuild a sane society.

One can also make reference to the relationship of Master and Apprentice, that reached its height at the time of the great guilds in 16th and 17th century Europe. The apprentices chosen to study under the master craftsman or painter partook of the wisdom and skill of this being. The master gained through his relationship with the fertile mind of enquiring youth.

Today, we should make a start by encouraging our smaller, quality oriented enterprises, to act in the same spirit. As this will not happen without a significant push, it is important to lay the foundation within the decentralised local and regional economics that are the starting point for all the actions proposed in this book.

It is in the domain of agriculture and artisan skills that the most pressing need exists to reorder and revive the relationship 'youth meets wisdom'. This is due to the critical state of breakdown in the system which trains young people to become tomorrow's skilled craftsmen and farmers. Without skilled craftsmen and farmers, there will be no proper food or tools. In the UK for example, the average age of the working farmer is now 59 years, and all over the developed world the mean age of farmers is creeping up. The great majority of young people are simply not interested in taking on the challenges of this profession, associated as it is with relatively low financial rewards (apart from the largest and most ruthlessly managed enterprises) and long hours on the land.

But we are in a time of great change, one mostly forced upon us due to the rapidly approaching collapse of our planetary resources.

Young people, attracted by an ecological and environmentally friendly philosophy of life, are venturing into territories once solely considered the domain of those with a lifelong commitment to farming, those born and bred on the land. Organic, biodynamic, permaculture, and generally ecological methods of farming, are emerging as the main vehicles for attracting young people into the countryside.

Tied into the challenges to develop renewable energy technologies and utilise novel (natural) building materials, the more entrepreneurial individuals are genuinely excited by the challenge that is at hand. However, the breakdown of genuine and sustainable farming and craft guilds, where the enthusiastic newcomer can learn from the wise practitioner, has exposed a great communication gap. A large link is missing form the chain – a link as vital as the land itself.

For the older, experienced practitioner, the gap brings with it a profound sense of loss. When one's own family have rejected the life of the land or the craftsman's trade, and no newcomers are knocking on the door, a sense of futility tends to outweigh the sense of achievement and a not easily overcome sadness tends to prevail. The solution on the agricultural level will be to bring together willing farmers, landowners and local authorities to devise together a scheme whereby young and aspiring growers or farmers have the opportunity to learn the rudiments of good land management and basic building skills.

The farmers most clearly suited to taking on the task of educators will be those who practise traditional and organic rotational farming methods: returning animal manures to the land and caring for their livestock in a humane and thoughtful way. What we call 'mixed farms'. The term means farms that combine a diversity of activities, incorporating farm animals, varied crops and grass or herb meadows. Such farms may use some extra synthetic inputs from time to time, but just because this cannot be categorised as strictly organic, this does not mean that they are sinners. There is much to be learned from the farmers who run these enterprises, and for the novice, a grounding in the rigours of mixed farming practices will stand them in good stead for whatever is to follow.

Young people should come as volunteers for the first year, and after that an appropriate financial return agreed, depending on the level of commitment and capability demonstrated. Such a hands-on experience is far more meaningful than years spent absorbing specialist information from books and college teachers. The farmer has the reward of being asked to expound and demonstrate his knowledge, to someone who really needs such a grounding. Local authorities should provide a stipend to the farmer during this process, as he or she is truly a teacher and should be rewarded accordingly.

A second way of developing the relationship 'youth meets wisdom' is for the farmer to open up a small area of land for the young person to try his or her hand at food growing, and/or renewable energy production plus basic shelter construction. Let us say ½ acre to start with. A nominal rent for the use of this land could be asked, and some local lodgings would have to be found by the student in cooperation with the farmer. The farmer would be able to advise the student about basic methods of food production – on a semi-informal level. The young person's questions could be discussed and solutions found.

Slowly the student will gain a feel for the land, the operations of the farm (good or bad) and the life of a farming family. Some small roots can be put down. The farmer will find himself or herself face to face with the reality of our time: an urban influenced individual reflecting that way of life, but seeking to go beyond at least some of its trappings and gain a working knowledge of how to grow food and deal with some of the issues of rudimentary self-sufficiency.

The fact is that this meeting has to take place, as there is no other plausible solution available to us. Increasingly large numbers of people will leave cities now, for the simple reason that most cities cannot sustain the levels of clean water and clean air demanded of them.

All cities of over around 200,000 populations will have to find drastic resolutions to their super consumptive lifestyles – and this cannot happen overnight. (See Chapter 15-Greening the City) Those able to perceive this and feeling a certain calling of the land will form the advance guard of urban refugees and heralds of a much larger influx to follow. *Farmers and landowners must be open to accommodating their needs, and local authorities must also fully engage in this process.*

Farmers no longer able to sell their commodities profitably in the global market should consider breaking down their larger fields into small scale units, planted to diverse crops, as a direct response to local demand. Such units could also be let to newcomers who have the desire to graduate into responsible growers and to develop their skills.[6]

Local authorities have a special responsibility to ensure that low impact housing schemes are given proper scope, and that planning permission is not blocked when good schemes are put forward. There is a pressing need for ecologically friendly shelter construction, essential to the broader success of reintegrating youth onto the land. It is the only way to avoid chaos once the position reaches a real crisis point, and people panic because food and water supplies dry up and poor air quality renders respiratory diseases endemic. At current rates of uninterrupted consumption levels, that time will come sooner rather than later; possibly very soon. We have to prepare for it now.

The urgency associated with reorganisation of vocational, hands-on experience on a large scale, requires that the

---

6 The UK journal 'The Land', www.tlio.org.uk, is worth exploring on this.

country is put on a 'War Footing'. That would be a socio-economic reorganizational plan comparable to those put into effect during World War II in the UK and elsewhere, under the 'dig for victory' campaign. The 'enemy' this time is less clear cut, but the danger is as, if not even more, acute. Now the enemy is ourselves, not another invader and not an outside terrorist organisation. It is only our own lack of willingness to face reality and to become genuinely aware that is preventing serious action being taken now – to avert a large scale crisis and to lay the foundations for the realisation of a genuinely sustainable way of life.

Youth Meets Wisdom is not a fabricated utopian ideal, but the most realistic and organic level of education available to us. It is full of joyous potential and hope. To ascribe elders to a 'past their sell-by date' dumping ground in special institutions, divorced from the daily interaction of society is a terrible waste of life. Except in cases where some specialised care is required, it amounts to a repetition of the way we treat our planet as a whole. Now a new chapter is beginning, and our respect and love for the fruits that come with age must be the bedrock upon which the new chapter is built.

11. Health and Medicine Towards a Universal State of Balance

What is health?

Some may say 'the absence of disease', but clearly this falls far wide of the mark. A state of well being? Certainly, that is not to be denied. But let us say more: an overall state of dynamic balance in mind, body and spirit.

Universal health is expressed as an overall state of dynamic balance throughout the universe.

But what is 'dynamic balance'?

'Balance' is expressed as a pivotal point between two extremes. It is a dynamic, resonant and 'centred' state of Being. One might also describe it as 'pure economy of movement'.

At the cosmic level, the 'equilibrium of balance' comes about as a result of charged particles emerging in a pivotal position between the energetic forces of attraction and repulsion. Equilibrium (health) is the light energy emerging out of the friction generated by these two forces. It (health) is an uninhibited energy that radiates both inwards and outwards simultaneously. It radiates out in all directions at once, (see the illustration of the chapters at the beginning of this book) causing a glowing incandescence to hover where it is expressed.

We on earth are part of this dynamic universal energy and we are aspiring participants in the Universal quest to find this state of true balance, true equilibrium: a state of enlightenment (being 'lit up').

That is to say, we share with the great cosmic spirit or spirits, the desire to realise that which is our potentiality: *to fully realise ourselves.* This is the drama of life's journey; it is at once our starting point and our goal. At the quivering 'pivotal point' of equilibrium, there is no difference between the alpha and omega points, they are subsumed into one vibrant, ever present entity.

For us, this life journey is not just a straight line between A and B. It is more what the poet William Blake called "the crooked road of genius". In fact, there can be no straight line in our universe – everything, as Einstein and others have observed, is on a curve. Even light energy bends its way around the planets as it makes its way to earth.

'Roundness' is the shape of our world, the planets and the great universal design of which we are all a part. It is also in the nature of energy to oscillate as it travels – a 'wave' movement – recognised, and intensely studied, by the quantum physicists in their probing of the behaviour of the minutest visible levels of matter. Ultimately, these minute particles of energy/matter were observed to transform themselves between specks of matter, waves, and what was described as 'a dance'.

The description of the subatomic particles participating in 'a dance' was a rather remarkable 'scientific' discovery – and demonstrates how even the very building blocks of life are taken up in artistic exigencies!

And that is surely the essence of it: we are but one special expression of a shared cosmic energy. We are born in the image of our Creator, thus we share with our Creator the conscious and ongoing exploration – and realisation – of all potential contained within us. *Thus the true expression of health is to be found in a manifestation of our oneness with balanced universal energies.*

What is disease?

It is literally a state of 'dis-ease', meaning: a state of 'not being at ease'. When we are not at ease with ourselves (and with our Creator) – we are out of balance. When we are out of balance, we experience anxiety, stress and depression. Essentially, we are 'not at ease with ourselves' when cut off from, or out of tune with, the dynamic of universal energy, as described above.

Such a condition expresses itself physically, as a malfunctioning of various organs of the body. Typically, heart and lungs, as well as the dispersal organs, including kidneys and liver. On the mental plain, it is expressed as a malfunctioning of mental equilibrium.

It is very helpful that the word 'dis-ease' so clearly gets to the quick of the matter. Being 'at ease' suggests being in harmony with the rhythm and flow of a greater macrocosmic energy. Not surprisingly, today, many are in search of this mysterious universal rhythm, finding in it a direct counterbalance to the fragmented and often stress laden lifestyles so many have felt impelled to adopt.

However, to be at ease for anything other than ephemeral bursts, involves a significant effort and ultimately, a substantial reward. It involves changing our way of life, and helping to change the way of life around us. It involves more inner fire and less unbridled ego; more spirit and less materialism; more introspection and less arrogance. It is a journey we all must embark upon if we are to realise 'true health', and if we are to minimise the state of disease: in ourselves, in our environment, and in our society as a whole.

It's all the same energy, but operating on different planes and at different frequencies.

So when we are concerned about human health, we should always first set that concern in the macrocosmic, universal context – from where it originated. The problem is that in the majority of cases we don't.

We are primarily concerned about ourselves – seen as divorced and separate from nature and the greater whole. This means that we are already starting from a position of 'disequilibrium' and in this situation it is only possible to speak about preventing or curing one *particular* illness or unhealthy trait, within a greater sphere of overall sickness. In medical terms, this is largely the role played by allopathic medicine, which has (in some cases) been remarkably efficient in this monocultural approach to treatment. Symptoms emerge, illness strikes, and a solution to reducing and/or removing that illness is often found. This has been particularly true in treating the rampant spread of certain viral diseases.

But not always of course. Pathogens become increasingly sophisticated in their ability to overcome medicines, just as bugs become immune to pesticides in agriculture, and the cat and mouse game between disease and cure continues indefinitely.

This might be considered an almost acceptable resolution, if it were not for the fact that the human body takes a hit each time such medicines are dispensed. Just as the living soil takes a bit each time it receives a dose of chemical input. This is because the composition of these medicines incorporates synthetic elements that, while helping to eradicate the particular problem they are designed to deal with, load other areas of the body with an excess of chemical components that put stress on the organs that must in turn try to deal with them. These medicines, after excretion, ultimately land up in the environment, causing pollution of ground water, soils, streams and rivers. They are known to have caused fish to change sex and to promote algae that smother out oxygen.

They can also get into our drinking water, thus ensuring a prophylactic cocktail of unwanted medicinal chemicals in our daily diet.

Allopathic medicine's weakness, however, is to be found in its reticence to treat symptoms of disease – rather than just its end manifestation. Similar to the farmer who relies on agro-chemical pesticides to suppress disease in his unsustainable monoculturally managed fields.

Driving the vast empire of patented 'pharma' medical treatments often adopted by allopathic doctors is the pathogenic desire to *control* people's health and dietary habits for profit: to make individuals parasitically dependent upon purchasing the 'cures' they produce. In other words, to keep society just sick enough to enable the coffers of pharma empires to be continuously replenished. In our daily diet, every food additive, colour, preservative and flavour enhancer is a tool for repressing and weighing down our natural health. All long shelf life food and undue food processing drains dynamic energy values and renders foods, and us, partially crippled. All agribusiness hybridisation of native seeds for the sole purpose of increasing yields, destroys a component of the subtle living energies that have been acquired over thousands of years of climatic and environmental adaptation. All synthetic vitamins and nutrients pharmaceutically concocted to become virtual supplements add small components of poison to our bodies and cannot provide the curative energies to be found in the foods provided directly by nature. Purchasing or being prescribed de-vitaminised, processed and altered foods and pills keeps the pharma empires *in control* of our health and leaves us *out of control*. Our health, it seems, is largely in the hands of those who profit by our illness. We are effectively 'dumbed down' by retaining dependency on such regimes; our subtle metabolism, creative thinking process and joie de vivre are held back and impaired – and therefore so our judgement and independence.

Within the world of formalised medicines, more humane, caring, time honoured and beneficial treatments manage to raise their heads. Homeopathic treatments base themselves on a macrocosmic, universal health reality. They do this by treating the 'whole person', seeing in her or him a complex interconnected dynamic composed of hundreds of inherently related elements all reacting and inter-reacting with each other at all times. Ayurvedic (Indian) and many Chinese practices are also founded in this 'whole person' analysis and care approach. Both demonstrate a highly sophisticated, age old, yet somehow absolutely contemporary understanding of the subtle vibratory levels that pervade the human condition. They utilise herbal and mineral components in their treatments that have no adverse side effects on the human body or the wider environment.

Such approaches also take into account mental and physical states: mind as well as body. Psychologists and psychiatrists are trained to 'heal the psyche', but this still represents only one component of our overall health.

Let me quote a short excerpt from a book by Maya Tiwari entitled 'Ayurveda Secrets of Healing': "Three primordial forces, or principles, interweaving to create five elements –space, air, fire, water, earth– give birth to the entirety of creation. The principle of stillness, 'tamas', replenishes the universe and its being and is the main principle and support within the physical universe and human life. The principle of harmonic and cosmic intelligence, 'sattra', maintains universal and individual stasis and awareness.

The three cosmic principles, called 'gunas' operating through the five elements they have created, directly interphase with human existence."

I do not mean to convey the message that western medicine's more specialist approach is wholly misguided; this would be a wrong interpretation. However allopathic medicine only finds meaning as a last resort remedy, as one remedial tool within the greater medical tool box. In its failure to look at the whole person, western medicine misses the universal health's bigger picture, which is essential for maintaining the long term health of body, mind and spirit. This has already been dealt with in earlier chapters.

But it is outside the realm of professional medical knowledge that the most widespread variety of health promoting formulae exists. At the grass roots, informal level, every culture in the world has a great storehouse of tried and tested treatments. Treatments very closely correlated with the native plants, herbs, trees and minerals that make up the local habitat. Tens of thousands of combinations, concoctions and potions are utilised, drawing from a native wisdom going back hundreds, if not thousands of years. The world's peasant farmers retain a great storehouse of knowledge concerning the attributes of these precious herbs, plants, trees and even minerals. They are the last guardians of our 'managed' naturesourced medicinal heritage.

Such cures are intimately connected with the intricate biodiversity of each region. Lose the biodiversity, and one loses the means of healing – and we just about have. A rich foundation of flora and fauna is at the root of widespread good health; and we are the primary managers of this biodiversity and main recipients of its bounty. *It is our responsibility – and nobody else's – to ensure the vital balance of all flora, fauna and soils on our planet. Even if this means leaving alone certain wildernesses (such as the world's rain forests) that are an abundant source of as yet unrecognised flora and a vast storehouse of potential cures to the illnesses that ravage our planet.*

Mismanagement, exploitation without giving back in return; pollution, and a general 'couldn't care less' attitude, constitute crassly bad practice, and a shameful refusal to recognise our wider universal responsibilities to look after and nurture good health in all that is precious. Negative and cynical thinking is itself a disease, as well as an invasive pollutant. Everything good in life stems and starts from trying to take a positive and caring attitude and encouraging the same in others.

Microcosm and macrocosm are two parts of one whole. A small cosmos: our planet and biosphere – and a big cosmos: our universe and beyond, reflect each other. If the earth is made sick by our bad habits, so will the greater universe of which the earth is a part, take-on a part of that sickness. If the universe becomes sick, so will the earth and so will man. *We are subject to the law of cause and effect and cannot break out of this 'bounce' unless, and until, the laws of man harmonise with universal laws.* It is supposed to be the purpose of universities ('universe-ities') to teach this, and it should be the primary role of our hospital service to practise it.

We will only cure ourselves, our planet and our universe through recognising our inseparable mutual interdependence, and by accompanying this recognition with consistent good practice and good discipline. This way we will discover 'Health' – perhaps for the first time.

Resolutions:

Starting at the local and regional level:
1. Find best practitioners with good knowledge of herbal health cures, and where to find best wild and cultivated plants and minerals.

2. Start local clinics based on the application of this knowledge.

3. Attract trained doctors with awareness of how to treat the 'whole person' – holistic medicine. Also homeopathic, ayurvedic and Chinese skills.

4. Draw in a local GP seeking to widen his or her field of knowledge. Encourage good communication between allopathic and holistic healers.

5. Raise the health awareness of the community in line with the points raised in this chapter.

6. Build awareness concerning the superior nutritional and health giving values of local, fresh, flavourful and seasonal, ecologically raised and wild foods. Remember: when it comes to illness, prevention is better than cure.

7. Ensure that all local drinking water is of the highest achievable quality.

8. Ensure that spiritual sensitivities are respected and built upon.

9. Find a good balance between physically and mentally demanding activities and genuine relaxation. Fresh air, exercise and a positive frame of mind, form the time honoured foundation of basic physical and mental health.

10. Build into all human relationships awareness, respect and compassion.

11. Completely redesign hospitals to be places of beauty, peace and tranquillity; and make holistic as well as allopathic treatment available for all patients.

12. Ensure that hospitals are supplied with good quality fresh foods.

12. Universal Law, Order and Justice

"Our lives begin to end the day we become silent about the things that matter." Martin Luther King

All controls are essentially a compensation for trust. With absolute trust between all, natural justice would prevail without the need for judicial laws.

The terrestrial model for community law, order and justice has its origins in tribal communities led by elders and village chiefs. However, it finds its most common expression even to this day within the family: fathers, mothers, sons and daughters (the family unit) is the first testing ground for order, discipline, punishment and reward.

As tribal communities evolved into fiefdoms, monarchies and eventually nation states, so too did the practical application of law, order and justice evolve. Within military regimes, law is only maintained by the most rudimentary levels of repression, a state of affairs still widely in evidence around the world today. The form such repression takes is based entirely upon the whim of the dictatorships and oligarchs who hold the reins of power.

Monarchies, introducing at least a measure of 'top down' justice, eventually superseded most military regimes; kings and queens becoming the new commanders-in-chief and establishing their particular favoured conditions for law, order and justice.

It has only been in the last six hundred years (in European history) that so-called parliamentary 'democratic' procedures finally broke through, and a clear framework for the administration of law and order became widely established. The precedent for this (in the UK) was King John putting his seal of approval on the right to 'trial by jury' and 'no detention without charge' in 1215, under the jurisdiction of the Magna Carta. However, by and large, judicial and jury systems, magistrates, law courts and appeal procedures are a very recent development.

Police forces, established to ensure that state laws are respected, find their origins in the establishment of the 'Polis' of ancient Greek society, in the time of Socrates and Plato. So the need to have a way of ensuring that the State was well run gave birth to 'the police'. To this day, the police have essentially the same role, maintenance of law and order in society. However, today in the UK and in the rest of Europe, the police and the courts come under the direct authority of parliament and its elected head, and, lest we forget, it is we who elect our parliamentarians and pay for our judicial system and police force operations.

In the 21st century our system of law, order and justice largely protects –and reflects– **our profoundly** materialistic scale of values. The system primarily stands for the defence of private property, acquired wealth and the status quo, as prescribed by the parliament of the day.

In truth, it was essentially little different during Plato and Aristotle's era: however the Polis of that time aspired to plead with, and take note of, the voice of the gods who so influenced Athenian and ancient Greek culture. Apollo, Dionysus and Aphrodite were frequently called upon to give direction to support those who ran the state, as well as to provide a degree of prophetic universal oversight for the propitious unfolding of daily life.

However, such universality of cosmic discipline is not to be found today. Our system is bereft of a deeper search for truth and guidance, however misguided. In fact, the law today is wholly divorced from any latent connection with the Laws of Nature or the Laws of the Universe. We ridicule any such correlation as spiritual hot air, or the ravings of demented souls. Is it any wonder, then, that law and order is breaking down, within such an implacably atheistic mindset?

All acts of law have their origin in Universal Law. The law of cause and effect, the law of cosmic balance, the law of gravity. So we have had to work hard over the last millennia to cut out such universal truth in our wholly terrestrial interpretations, and come up instead with something which acts primarily as a largely unsubtle tool for the protection of wealth, power, privilege and property.

This is not to say that within the court systems of Europe, individual judgements are not, at times (depending on who is 'sitting') based on a bolder and more humanistic assessment of the predicament under scrutiny. There are examples when it is. However, judges and juries are confined to operating within the generally accepted norms of the status quo, and the full range of limitations that comes with it.

Moral, ethical and universal calls for help are largely dispatched as irrelevant within a society firmly locked into protecting its own blinkered self-interest. In recent times, this self-interest has also been behind an alarming and insidious erosion of civil rights. Taking the UK as an example, the country now has one CCTV camera for every fourteen people; a huge government instigated DNA data base which can be used to pry into millions of innocent people's lives, and an ever lengthening period of detention (arrest) for anyone 'suspected' of terrorist interests. All these increasingly invasive actions have been taken through parliament on the back of intense propaganda concerning the supposedly ever present 'threat of terrorism'. It is now illegal to stand outside the Houses of Parliament and (in any way) publicly decry the invasion of Iraq. We have reached the point where the lines cast by Bob Dylan in the late 1960s now resonate increasingly strongly: "to live outside the law – you have to be honest".

If one wishes to pronounce upon large scale miscarriages of justice, such as indefensible invasions of foreign countries and the murder of their citizens, should it be a crime to stand outside the Houses of Parliament and articulate this?

Can one truly be accused of promoting 'terrorism' through taking a peaceful stand against unwarranted acts of violence?

If the laws of man fail to protect those who protect nature – and man – against destruction by corporate greed, and instead defend governments who depend upon these corporations' money in order to retain power – is it then wrong to step outside the legally executed lie, and act in defence of that upon which all life depends? Of course not, it is the only responsible thing to do under the circumstances. Civil disobedience is essential when 'obedience' amounts to becoming an accomplice to gross irresponsibility.

When the status quo has only its own vested interests to defend, it always accuses those who have some moral fibre of wishing to disrupt the smooth operation of its own indefensible terrorist activities. The law is increasingly being used as a blunt instrument in the defence of the indefensible. When those who fight for deeper justice are blatantly obstructed in their efforts, the 'citizen's arrest' of those who lie at the bottom of such iniquities, becomes our last resort in upholding a deeper, humanitarian driven level of justice.

The European Convention on Human Rights constitutes a basic safety net against blatant contravention of civil liberties. However, it fails to address or explore the deeper significance of true justice, allowing space for political manipulation of the system for end goals which serve to maintain vested interests, rather than serving the basic needs of the majority of people.

A legally constituted Global Charter of Human Rights, admirable as the idea is, is still a way off; and in the vacuum created by its absence, we have to take life into our own hands *and recreate a just society*, starting at the regional level.

The 'Just County', 'Just District' or 'Just Parish' is a good starting point. Initially small collective actions, offering a solid defence against the further erosion of basic community values, can be the starting point. The interconnection of many 'Just Counties' will eventually bring hope to the lives of millions, presently unable to achieve or enjoy responsible citizenship within the lottery of a system that is quick to fine or gaol those who fail to follow its ultimately self-defeating goals.

But we have to be careful: there is nothing inherently benign about localised initiatives; they depend for their success upon the fact that those who participate in them do not harbour ambitions to become 'little kings' (or little queens) within their own communities. One must be ever watchful and snuff out such tendencies before they get started.

The proper conditions for devising just laws, and the just application of such laws, at the regional level and beyond, require that we become receptive to the principles that govern universal laws and the laws of nature. Man-made laws, that have completely divorced themselves from this sphere of influence can (as we see) only cause harm; and unless rectified, ultimately lead to the destruction of our entire planetary life resource base and all human values. *Laws that support working against nature have run their destructive course, and we have no choice but to start again, this time guided by the greater law we have so far consistently denied.*

So, as if coming around on some vast spiral voyage, we now pass again over the early manifestations of community law, order and justice, as administered by tribal elders and village chiefs; casting a respectful but wary eye their way.

Just like the plume that streams out behind a comet on its vast circular journey, we carry with us the knowledge and memory of this early phase of our social evolution, and can once again draw upon it in establishing a further evolved system of inclusive, humanitarian, law, order and justice. One which binds universal laws with the laws of man, through a process which ensures that they form a happy marriage and a joyous complementarity.

Once a collectively devised system of localised justice has come up to speed and attained a certain critical mass, national and international governance will become more widely influenced, and will eventually become integrated into an unstoppable process of change. The final phase of this process will be to bring to birth a legally recognised form of World Charter for Peace and Justice, whose benign influence will eventually reach into all corners of the world, and complement the local and regional self-governance programmes that this book seeks to set in motion. A new world order will be ushered into being; governed by a constantly evolving 'universal' understanding of the process of law, order and justice.

The military – as protectors

Under the terms of modern day governance, the armed forces are not given direct responsibility for the maintenance of civil laws. The army, navy and air force, also coming under the jurisdiction of parliament, have the task of maintaining the broader peace, via defending the nation state against attack or invasion from outside. The military are also called to act upon parliamentary decisions and agreements that they themselves may feel less than enthusiastic about; such as to enter foreign territories in order to wage war, put down supposedly repressive regimes, and shoot to kill when commanded.

There is a strong case to be made for the forces adopting a non-cooperation policy when ordered to carry out a clearly vindictive or entirely inappropriate mission; such as one calling for death and destruction to be perpetrated on fellow human beings who have not been genuinely identified as posing a threat to the nation in question.

Armies, navies and air forces also have an increasingly important role in helping out at times of national disasters and weather related crises. Many individuals in the forces feel more inclined to protect life rather than to take it. The armed forces are the outer skin or shield that protects countries in emergencies, and ensure that countries can resist attempts to overthrow them by murderous conspirators.

We should not view the army, navy and air force as merely institutions of war, any more than we should view the police force as purely an institution of repression. There are many very able, caring and courageous individuals who join the ranks, and their strengths can be seen first hand when a genuine crisis strikes a nation and they are called in to help people find shelter and protection.

In building our decentralised, self-autonomous regional communities, we will need to garner the respect and cooperation of both the armed forces and the police. Many are already finding it increasingly difficult to offer their services to countries run by thoughtless and inhumane political figureheads. They have a certain pride. I believe we will need our forces for some time yet. Indeed, we may well need their protection and support when times get tough, and our fledgling new society attracts the attention of those determined to retain their power base at any price.

Breaking the law – justice as a source of healing

When basic justice is callously ignored, steps need to be taken to ensure that the individuals concerned come to truly recognise their errors, as a precondition for re-entering and contributing to the rhythm of a community's daily life. But the punishment should be appropriate to the crime. In many cases, an enforced period of workbased rehabilitation overseen by a senior member of the community can provide a positive stepping stone on the road to a cure.

If someone steals from someone else, then the reciprocal action required is for the one who perpetrated the crime to give back something more than they took, in whatever way or form is deemed most suitable. We should always first examine the circumstances of the crime. For example, if someone steals because of a genuine need or lack, it is different than stealing for motives based on greed.

In the Just Society, the community should always ensure that its inhabitants are not so impoverished as to feel constantly tempted to make amends through antisocial behaviour. That is the primary task of any community. All should play a part in ensuring the overall health and welfare of the community; all should take an interest in peace and justice; all should be part of devising ways to maintain the constant equilibrium and enhancement of life at all levels. However, thoughtful elders and the genuinely wise – so long as they practise as they preach – remain the best jurors, councillors and administrators of local justice, and ultimately also national justice.

Those who have this responsibility, also have the responsibility of ensuring that a far going form of justice is administered. *Here I refer to justice as a process of healing, as in the healing of a sickness, and as such, not a punishment at all.* Such a healing process involves inducing a mending of ways, or a return to the path which has been lost or deviated from.

Only by being attuned to higher universal laws can a man or woman administer genuine justice. Only the application of universal laws can guide those who administer justice to find the right remedial healing process. So the very real skills involved in judicial decision making should be recognised as crucial in maintaining a state of balance and harmony within the community, region, state and world.

The steps taken to encourage the deviant back into his or her proper role in community life may well involve such individuals spending time with a number of caring citizens holding different skills; but the offender –to be truly healed– must ultimately recognise the beneficial value of this process – and be truly grateful for it.

Very serious crimes, like murder or grievous bodily harm, will become a thing of the past in communities operating a system of justice that balances human and universal laws. Digging deep into self-awareness, holistic and lateral thinking, and allowing compassionate feelings for the trials and tribulations of all fellow citizens, this is the real meaning of being just and responsible: being 'able to respond'.

Our 21st century overcrowded and overstretched prison services provide no answer to redressing criminality within society. They merely postpone the need to address the real problem lying at the root of all seriously antisocial and inhuman behaviour: that the standards of so-called civilised societies are themselves riddled with injustice, coercion and deceit. Through the reintegration of society into a brocade of thousands of Just Parishes and broadly self-governing regions, genuine justice can be reawakened, reapplied and eventually celebrated as a profoundly significant expression of human kind.

This is not to suggest that present parish communities are in some mysterious way 'paradigms of virtue', free from vice and connivance. Far from it, many are microcosmic political hotbeds and highly fractious.

As in all issues covered in this book, it is the potential which is our concern. When the scale is small and the community is genuinely concerned about its welfare, we have the best possibility of learning to treat each other like members of an extended family, rather than anonymous strangers.

The foundations of a humane society start in a caring community, so does the administration of a life affirmative system of justice.

13. Governments, Corporations and Globalisation

Successive governments have consistently demonstrated that they lack the vision or capacity to steer society in a benign and responsible direction. Levels of corruption and mishandled authority are endemic throughout our world today, and it has got to the point where our creative energies are better utilised in building a new ship than trying to repair the old one.

In a world battered by political, religious and economic violence it is hard to come to terms with the fact that we are nevertheless, at bottom, united by our common identity as human beings. Whatever our colour or creed, we all share the same basic needs and common aspirations.

Seen from the perspective of some angelic host flying in from another dimension, our divisive behaviour must seem extraordinarily stupid. Such beings must surely wonder why we should appear so determined not only to hurt, maim and kill each other, but to also do the same to our home – that slowly revolving jewel called Planet Earth.

Leaving, as we do, the main earthly management tasks to self-interested government institutions and business corporations, we then express surprise, anger and cynicism, when the job of managing society is not being well done and 'democracy' appears to be failing in just about all spheres.

Most government uses of our taxable income and capital are not channelled into easily identifiable life improvement projects for the benefit of those most in need, but into grand schemes primarily designed to generate ever greater taxable revenue from corporate profits, encouraging the process of further fattening already well-lined pockets.

Banking systems act as the agents for reinvestment of most commercially viable private sector earnings. Mostly we have no idea where our funds are placed once deposited in the bank of our choice. Essentially we have lost control over our savings the minute we open our bank accounts. But it's a fair guess to assume our money is lumped into the massive investment funds that provide loans to giant corporate and government projects, such as motorway and airport building projects, power stations, agro-chemical and pharmaceutical conglomerates, genetic engineering research and development projects, the weapons trade, including nuclear weapons... and so on.

Such enterprises are not geographically confined to the country where the money is invested, they are global investments. So we can unwittingly be supporting the building of a huge and highly controversial dam on the Namada River in India, or a vast shopping mall in Bali; a highly polluting aluminium smelting plant in Iceland; a US petroleum corporation in Iraq; or a pig factory farming complex in Poland.

Considering the way most of our money is being used, we are basically giving the banks a licence to kill: a global licence to kill.

Transnational and multinational corporations pretty much rule in today's world. When the wages they pay their workers are deemed too costly, they shift to countries where the minimum wage is twelve times lower than the European and North American average, and only just above that nation's poverty line. That has the effect of holding down the price of the manufactured item to so-called 'competitive' levels in the post-industrial countries who are the beneficiaries of the end product.

Building a Honda car in India will cost one twelfth of what it would cost to build in the UK, but the price of the car will not be twelve times cheaper than in the UK, just not quite as expensive as a competitor's similar style model. In order to remain viable, the competitor then feels obliged to undercut his rival and heads off to China to get a deal together which will ultimately lead to his corporation's car being produced under an even lower workers wage.

Over and over again, under the aegis of stimulating the world economy or the national gross domestic product, small scale independent economies are driven to bankruptcy, communities destroyed and individuals forced into virtual slavery by the sheer size and power of the dominant global corporate players, who step on and shove aside all and sundry in their unquenchable obsession with power and profit.

Industrial scale globalisation is a rampantly profit driven and largely ruthless process. We remain its advocates up until the moment when we cease to give carte blanche to our banks, insurance companies and governments, to use our investments and savings to continue to fuel this process. As it is, they are no doubt delighted by the fact that we rarely ask any questions, except 'how much interest will I earn?'

If we want to make a difference, we have no choice but to remove our money from institutions that support the forces of destruction.

In the retail industry, supermarket chains are the master exploiters of our acquisitive weakness. These transnational corporations play on the western bargain hunting obsessions and, under the basic premise of 'pile it high, sell it cheap' , they contract the poorest farmers of the world to mass-produce their stock-in-trade items at the cheapest possible prices, and to an exacting formula; one that allows for no blemishes or remotely non conformist shapes and sizes.

Such a formula is only achievable by using heavy doses of specific agro-chemicals and/or genetic modification techniques, both of which destroy the soil and the living biodiversity of the area under cultivation. The very same soil and environment which these native farmers rely on to meet their own families' subsistence food needs. Independent family farms are thus subjugated into becoming the servants of industrial globalisation.

So next time you feel a sense of revolt when seeing a picture of a vast treeless monocultural prairie in the midwest of the USA, the Polish plains, the Spanish Algarve or the Norfolk fens – or anywhere else for that matter, remember that we are paying for it because of a largely selfish desire for 'convenience' 'bargains' and 'supermarket assured' quality control regimes.

The next time you admire a nice piece of white cling film wrapped fillet of pork, or chicken in the supermarket chiller, remember that you already paid for it once, through enabling your bank to invest your money in the numerous utterly inhumane pig and poultry prisons strung out across the world. Prisons established with the sole purpose of ensuring that you get a bargain – and the supermarket a bigger profit –when you pay the second time for this sad tasteless piece of flesh at the store's till.

Governments receive a large share of their financial support from such corporations. It is, of course, a reciprocal arrangement. To keep their side of the bargain, government must ensure good conditions for its sponsors; it must smooth the way for a continuing improvement of profit margins, market dominance and good business terms.

Our governments, multinational corporations and state sponsored institutions such as the World Bank, International Monetary Fund and The World Trade Organisation are all part of the same club: a club determined to exact the last ounce of profit from the world's ever more depleted material and human resource base; all the while supported by our taxes and the money we put into the mainstream banking system.

Government and industrial globalisation go hand in hand. They have become an inseparable part of one vast sea of high level corruption. *It is therefore now necessary to put an end to our support for this rapacious process of destruction and re-align our money with that which enhances the health and welfare of people and the planet.*

Once we understand just how inhumanely and irresponsibly our investments are utilised, we can more easily make the decision to invest ethically, and accept a somewhat smaller monetary return, but gain a clearer insight into the end use being made of our assets. As stated in Chapter 2, ethical investment institutions (banks) are a good starting point for all those determined to no longer continue passively accepting being a party to irresponsible mainstream banking procedures.

The next step will be to start directly supporting the decentralised, positive local projects that form the foundation of the new community-led renaissance which is the theme of this book.

The process of weaning one's assets from the old destructive, to the new creative investment procedures is highly significant. *If such a transition is made at the rate of say, twenty five percent of one's banked assets per annum, the effect will be marked.* We will be cutting off funds to those who mismanage them, and at the same time giving support to people and projects destined to heal, nurture and restore our communities, regions and countries.

Once a critical mass of such responsible reinvestment has been attained, the world will quite literally start to change, and our unrealised hopes will steadily become a reality.

Once the momentum becomes unstoppable and the new renaissance has truly found its equilibrium, we will start to discover the meaning of a One World Community, a new globally aware society, born out of a common, shared love and respect for all that beautifies, enhances and nurtures the gift of life for which we are all trustees. Essentially, any form of indulgence in the 'nation state' does not stand up to scrutiny once examined in depth. Countries whose wealth is largely dependent upon callously exploiting the resources of others are hardly in a position to bang the national drum. And anyway, the national drum itself is now a tired and worn out instrument, lacking any real resonance. Nation states and their elected governments have finally run out of gas, or used up all the gas they were run on.

We, the electorate, are sick of the vacillations and posturings of our corporate controlled governments. We can no longer find any enthusiasm for this tired and corrupt old ship; which means something else has to take its place.

That, dear reader is where we make our entrance ... just as others make their exit. We step into the void left by the deflating model that preceded it. The transition is already under way.

However, it is in its infancy, and we have to make sure that it finds adequate momentum and scope so that it can stir and inspire a great new hope for the future, in all those able to recognise it.

14. The Transformation of Governments

Aristotle, when asked by a student why he did not run for government, replied that in order to gain significant political power, he would have to compromise so severely his personal integrity and quest for truth, that it would defeat the ultimate objective of attaining wise political leadership.

Clearly little has changed since 350 AD; such is the level of corruption, compromise and insincerity (masked as earnest commitment) in government today.

The task involved in bringing about the transformation of national government, follows on from the task of transforming local government under the reform process described in earlier chapters. National government will have far less influence over the daily lives of individual citizens once local and regional government have won back their authority.

A newly established self governing role of the regions will have effectively decentralised the decision making powers previously dictated by Westminster, and other national governments throughout Europe and beyond. Regional self autonomy will be well advanced.

However, there will be some issues of national and international importance which will remain in the domain of national parliament. These will include: defence, macro economics, policing (but not all), health (but not all), foreign affairs, immigration, international cooperation and long distance transport systems. Research and reform of the voting system will also have to be undertaken to reflect fulfilment of the steps necessary in bringing about a just society. A reconstituted national parliament will also need to ensure proper coordination and co-operation between the regions; in a similar vein to a conductor maintaining the unity and equilibrium of an orchestra.

The motivation of those seeking election will need to be very different from the current partisan allegiances that are the standard requirement for most political aspirants. The new situation will demand that those standing for election to central government are free from such prejudices and persuasions.

Instead, members of parliament will have to have developed a sufficiently evolved sense of humanity and wisdom to hold the needs of all the electorate in equal measure. At bottom, all humans share the same basic needs – and it is only through maintaining a forced disparity of wealth and class that divisions and injustices are created – and the attendant jealousies and resentments are fostered and played-out.

Overcoming these false divisions calls for an end to the 'party system' as we know it. No longer should there be the need for a party to broadly represent the labour force, white collar workers or the bourgeoise. No longer should there be the need for a party to represent the interests of any particular segment of society.

The categories themselves will dissolve as delineations of divisions in society are recognised as divisive and unconducive to an overall unity of purpose.

The new government will consist of elected officials deemed worthy of serving society thoughtfully, wisely and compassionately. The new parliament will have to move away from 'opposition' and elected party members, confrontationally facing each other across the chamber floor, as in the current Westminster design. Rather, parliamentary proceedings should take place within a circular or semi circular designed space, which is inclusive and speaks of a common dialogue and goal, benefiting the greater whole.

Ultimately, such national governing bodies should join up to form a World Parliament, whose edicts will centre around an examination and synthesis of humanities' (and all other living beings) collective and common needs.

Upper and Lower Houses will also lose their significance once the qualities of 'aristocracy' are recognised in 'commoners', and the quality of 'commoners' are recognised in 'aristocrats'.

However, before discarding the Upper House, we should give careful consideration to the value of retaining a second chamber composed of wise individuals who have a particular overview on the proceedings of daily life, and can bring their experience to bear whenever called upon to do so.

In the meantime, local self rule is essential to ensure against as yet unreformed central government factions attempting to wrest control over regional assets and resources such as water supplies, minerals and land capable of growing crops without synthetic fertilizers and pesticides. A plausible scenario in view of the impending oil, food and climate crisis facing all nations and the demagogic nature of those accustomed to holding the reins of power.

Compassionate, wise and pragmatic local and regional authorities are essential for the proper workings of regional and local government.

The reforms need to become well established across the regions, before national government can be transformed. The general transition from ineffective and ineffectual local administrations, to positively motivated and integrated local teams, needs to be completed within a three to four year period, ushering in a new era of collective hope and optimism.

15. Greening the City
Jumping in the Deep End

For many, 'direct actions' to redirect the resources of the community, will involve confronting the immediate reality surrounding the place where one lives, and in many cases this will be an urban environment. This will mean going 'head to head' with the seemingly indomitable task of greening one's cityscape. Is it possible?

When anything between one and eight million people live cheek by jowl, surrounded by concrete, tarmacadam, cars, buses, trains, deoxygenated air, sterile water and the perpetual cacophony of noise that accompanies the whole shebang, one can only wonder: how is it possible such edifices hold together and how do *people* hold together?

No simple answer of course. But one simple observation: all such conurbations are utterly reliant upon large volumes of outside resources to maintain their super-consumptive lifestyles. *They are heavily in debt to the global economy for their food, their energy and their financial wealth.*

London, for example, requires eighty percent of its food to be shipped and flown in from all over the world – and almost one hundred percent of its energy. Without the power of a massive oil based global economy to keep it fed and fuelled, London – and all other such metropolises – would be largely uninhabitable.

This is why it is hard to base my vision of a sustainable future in a big city landscape. The change required to make such places into genuinely sustainable, semi-self sufficient communities, is on the very outer limits of feasibility. This being the case, and faced by the reality of still expanding world megatropolises, declining oil availability, rising food prices, worsening pollution and the accompanying need to drastically cut back on CO_2 emissions, what on earth are we to do?

Many imaginative minds have set themselves to consider this question over the years, and numerous suggestions have emerged: but nothing has really changed – mainly because large cities are centres of power for magnates of the 'status quo', and the vested interests of these magnates tend only to allow a little 'green icing' to embellish their very un-green cake.

Those in the seats of power are quite masterful at giving an impression of caring about such environments and the health, social security and welfare of residents.

None of this, oddly enough, changes the notion that a genuine attempt to effect a 'greening of the city' is a pulsatingly exciting challenge, full of extraordinary possibility and a veritable carbon sink for human imagination and creativity.

So here is an 'off the cuff' overview response to this great challenge. An "If I was Mayor of London 'blueprint'".

Every main artery leading to and from the countryside should be planted up to become be tree lined from outside city limits right up to the central vortex. 'Green Avenues' psychologically and physically create a flow of fresh air, and connect up town and country: an essential prerequisite for a two way dialogue.

Every house proprietor, flat owner or tenant would be offered a financial incentive to use every available space i.e. window ledge, balcony, flat roof, terrace and earthy plot, to plant-up edible and colourful sweet smelling plants and flowers. Local authorities would be instructed to plant scented climbers at the base of drainpipes, street lamps and other appropriate utilitarian obelisks.

Within every borough (London is composed of scores of joined-up/interconnected villages) there would be a whole series of smallish community allotments, where fresh fruit and vegetables could be grown and green manuring could be practised, utilising vegetable waste matter from surrounding households as well as composted degradable local fibrous materials.

I would then offer incentives to reduce drastically all cars and trucks, at the same time setting in motion a wholesale shift to public transport based on electrification, hydrogen and other appropriate green technologies; but making bicycle transport and people-powered rickshaws the main means of short distance local transportation.

Potable water sources would be provided by filtered direct rainwater catchment technologies situated on roof tops, drain pipe catchment tanks and special multi purpose reservoirs (constructed in parks and park gardens) that would incorporate attractive water features and also serve as meditative 'calmers'.

Shops, restaurants, pubs and clubs would only be licensed if they could guarantee that a fifty percent energy reduction had been achieved in their premises and special rate reductions would be given to any that went further than this, or that switched to renewable energy.

All schools, hospitals and public institutions would be required to provide imaginative interior green spaces and menus and diets – of which over half the items must consist of fresh, regionally grown ecological produce. This produce would be delivered via environmentally friendly, medium to small scale transport systems using the least polluting non-fossil fuels available.

Parks, the great life saving lungs of most cities, would have special areas given over to demonstration plots showing how to best 'grow your own' foods and how to design imaginative productive plots for raising medicinal herbs and simple vitamin rich native fruits. Small scale 'City Farms', pioneered by heroic enthusiasts over the past three decades, would be greatly increased in number and directly linked to schools for hands-on experiences to be gained by all pupils, within programmes specifically introduced into the national curriculum.

I would introduce annual competitions in each urban borough to come up with the best practical resolutions to the outstanding socio-economic problems facing their communities. This would include residential businesses, schools and private citizens.

In the arts, I would encourage special competitions for community design features and events that stimulate the momentum for a new 'pride of place' to blossom amongst local citizens – including pluralistic expressions of modern cosmopolitan societies, creatively engaged in colourful cultural self expression. Street parties would also be on the agenda, especially when some particularly important achievement had been successfully concluded.

'Quality of life' initiatives would be placed at the centre of all financial incentives and at the heart of a massive metamorphosis of misplaced and misdirected human (and non human) energies, in which creative 'greening' opportunities would become the main source of new employment opportunities.

Ways should be found to encourage local businesses to take a significant role in providing interest free loans and outright philanthropic donations to all locally approved initiatives that support the renaissance of integrated, healthy, spirit lifting community actions. Especially those that put towns and cities on the road to a community survival plan, designed to address the necessity of change dynamically – and not stubbornly to deny it.

Surrounding farmland (which has not already been concreted over) will have at least a small degree of responsibility lifted from its shoulders in its role as main provider of food for the urban masses. And perhaps as importantly – will be physically and psychologically 'connected up' with the city as part of a common endeavour to re-establish some plausible form of regional food security, for what are inherently over-populated areas.

Around six million acres (2.5 million hectares) of surrounding farmland would be needed to supply London with basic national food security. According to the 'Proximity Principle' (see Chapter 4) this food should come from as close to the capital as possible. But the reality is that roads, airports, business developments and new housing estates have already eaten up most of the main quality food producing land around London – and the same increasingly applies to all large conurbations throughout the world. Designating land from further afield would mean eating into farmland needed to supply other urban centres in these regions, so this is not a viable option.

This puts the onus back on urban centres to develop some extraordinary in-house solutions to their futures. For example, in my new London, car parks freed-up by the drastic reduction of private cars, would be turned into multi layered food producing structures, incorporating sun tunnels, reflective panels and glass roofs. Initially imported soils would be laid down, but later composted recycled materials based on domestic green wastes would replace outside soil imports.

All shops would be forbidden from providing plastic bags to customers, and food shops would be prohibited from selling any more than twenty five percent of fresh produce in packaged or wrapped formats.

The ball would be set rolling with a highly publicised overall target to improve air quality by fifty percent over a five year period, together with a fifty percent reduction in fossil fuel consumption (domestic, business and transport) and a twenty five percent decrease of global food and energy imports within the same five year period. The overall objective will be to catalyse the great store of practical and creative human energy that remains largely untapped in all of us. This will lead to a renaissance of positive thinking – and acting – to meet the enormous challenges that lie ahead to green our cities.

*I*n Conclusion

"A journey of a thousand miles begins with a single step.
Lao-Tzu

This book strives to identify the main ingredients needed to form the properly laid foundations for a unified sense of creative purpose in our lives. It is intended as a tool for change.

The new society which we must usher into existence is not a fixed entity. It is a constantly evolving being – and we must lay out a formula for establishing the new roots which then have to be carefully nurtured and watered if they are to produce fine fruit.

The emergence of a critical mass of individuals willing and able to take responsibility for the future, will take place at the same time as the appearance of further failures of the present system to cope with the gathering repercussions of decades of prevarication and mismanagement. However, this should not detract from, but rather spur on, the momentum of urgent activities. It is a time of crossing over. A new life coming into being as an old life crumbles away.

There will surely be great, and unprecedented, geophysical and human tremors during this time: but we should not fear, as a great sickness cannot just disappear quietly. A high fever, which is what our earth is suffering through, has to be sweated out, and deeply embedded poisons have to be regurgitated to cleanse the body and purify the arteries. We can better cope with these upheavals if we recognise that

153

they are a necessary part of a greater process of change.

There is no magic pill to cure our planet or its people. However the more aware we become about the deep seated ills afflicting all realms of planetary life, the more ready we will be to shift the angle of our current trajectory, and embark on the new course. A course that leads beyond the ensuing chaos and into the new order which is our absolute prerogative to set in motion[7].

Julian Rose,
January 2009

---

7 For further ideas related to the implementation of actions suggested in this book, please see www.changingcourseforlife.info

$\mathbb{A}$ppendix
Letter to Polish Farmers

Dear Farmers,

For many, these are hard times. Hard, because right across the spectrum prices are down and costs are up. Because youngsters are not showing enthusiasm to follow on the work that you have given your lives to. Because farming appears to be grossly undervalued and food taken for granted.

But the most important issue facing us farmers is a broader one that underlies these concerns: *How can we overcome the increasing stranglehold of governments, corporations and supermarkets that combine to profit from our willingness to comply with their agendas?*

Farmers in England and in all other countries that joined the EU over the past 30 to 40 years, have had to fight the same battle that now confronts farmers in Poland. It is a battle with bureaucracy, with stifling rules and regulations, absurd hygiene and sanitary standards, and an increasingly unpredictable global market place. On top of this, you will have observed, that approximately 20% of farmers (the largest) get 80% of the financial rewards/subsidies. This reveals just how biased the whole system is. Biased in favour of large scale, monocultural, supermarket led agribusiness. *An agribusiness that needs only four or five milk processing plants in the whole country and one quarter of the slaughter houses and other food processing sites that serviced the provinces in the pre-EU years.*

The pressures exerted by this 'top down' big business regime are felt most acutely by family farms striving to compete with inhuman factory farming pig enterprises such as Smithfield and Danish Crown. To compete with cheap milk imports from surplus producing nations flooding an under-designated milk quota Polish market place; destroying the market for dairy farmers who have just been encouraged to 'get bigger and more efficient' in order to compete. To compete with the vast egg production concentration camps that cram 30,000 hens into sunless steel sheds and feed them on genetically modified soya beans and maize, to make sure that a completely unaware public gets its tasteless eggs cheap and fast. Then the producers of cereals, subjected to a chaotic price fluctuation from year to year and costs of production that are always rising. Farms that are stalked by Cargill salesmen, always ready to convince you that their seeds and feeds are better and cheaper than anyone else's... but not telling us how low the vitamin and nutrient levels contained in their modified seeds and how much one will need to rely on their range of pesticides in order to ensure a reasonable harvest.

All these issues, and many more besides, now face you. The very big farms don't worry, they do what they are told and get a big chunk of EU support for their compliance. But in so doing they destroy the soils that are the most vital asset of any nation. They become slaves to monocultural agribusiness and European Union pay-outs.

Is that the way you want to go? Do you long to be a lonely US style prairie farmer? Do you want to kill off the biodiversity of the land? Are you willing to be bought-out by foreign farming corporations?

This letter is to those who answer NO! To those who value the way of life that nurtures the land from generation to generation and who are sickened by the destruction caused by greed and short-sighted profiteering. It is not for those apologists who say "there's nothing we can do" so "what's the point in bothering". No, it is for those who DO CARE and are prepared to unite in order to ensure that a line is drawn and a better future is forged. A future that is NOT dependent upon foolish politicians and rip-off merchants, but on well organised groups of farmers and farmers' friends who genuinely care for the (rapidly eroding) quality of life that we know is the foundation of rural communities all over the world. BUT DO NOT, FOR A MINUTE, BELIEVE THAT THIS QUALITY OF LIFE WILL BE PRESERVED WITHOUT A BIG EFFORT BY US.

We do not have to become resigned to suffering the fate of state and corporate slavery. We have to come together. Because together we are very strong – at least 1,500,000 family farmers – producing some 20% of Polish gross domestic productivity.

However, it is not going to happen by going along to the union representative and asking him to ask government to do something about your problem. Most of the main unions are financially supported by government, they are tools of the corporate state. They support the 100 ha –and bigger– farms and the mass produced supermarket commodities that are wiping out small farmers all over the world.

So are you ready to get up off your sofas and form a farmer led resistance movement? Are you ready to say NO to those, both national and foreign, who relentlessly exploit your naivety? Will you defend your beautiful Poland – which I am privileged to live in – so that future generations will not be impoverished slaves working for Brussels and Warsaw bureaucrats?

Behind the technocrats and bureaucrats stand the global corporations: *it is their desire to control the entire human food chain.* Already, just 4 US corporations control more than 60% of the world's commercial seed enterprises. They do not want to stop at that. Increasingly they are patenting the seeds which they control and they are genetically modifying them as a way of claiming 'ownership'. They want us, the farmers, to purchase these GM seeds from them and pay them a royalty for the honour of doing so. And this is what millions of Indian farmers have been doing and why thousands are now taking their own lives because their harvests have failed and they have no money left to buy native seeds. It is a terrible tragedy. But the same tragedy is stalking at the door of Polish farmers.

In the US and in Canada, hundreds of farmers are facing large fines and prison sentences for unintentionally contravening Monsanto's rule book.

Behind the global corporations stand the World Trade Organisation, The International Monetary Fund, the United States Department of Agriculture, the World Health Organisation, The Food and Agricultural Organisation and various other vast impersonal institutions. Be aware, they are all in it together – and they want us out of the way.

The transnational corporations and the global control institutions: they are united in their common goal of profiteering under the banner of bringing reform, modernisation and 'new markets' to unsuspecting nations. In their eyes, Poland is one of these unsuspecting nations.

But our 'leaders' are not going to defend us or our countries against those wishing to steal our assets. They, like virtually all politicians, will placate and sooth your worries, but they will not actually deviate from the corporate agenda and the opportunistic career offers that beckon. They have, after all, already sold off the Polish cream to the highest bidders – and now they are trying to sell you off too.

In 2001, Jadwiga Lopata and I attended a Brussels European Commission meeting especially arranged for us by a senior Polish civil servant. It involved meeting the main negotiators of Poland's entry into the European Union Common Agricultural Policy. We were authentically told by the chairwoman at that meeting that it was the intention of the Commission to restructure and modernise Polish agriculture", and that to do this, it would be necessary to remove over 1 million Polish farmers from their holdings and encourage them to take jobs in the cities.

We protested that these farmers were needed on the land. But the only reaction was "The European Union is not interested in small farms."

It is vital to understand: the underlying policies of the European Union are anti farmer. In their eyes, farmers are for the mass production of commodities for the global market. They are useful only to the extent that they raise a nation's Gross Domestic Product (export earnings). It is not even a question of recognising farmers' essential role in guaranteeing national food security.

Not even that.

Good food quality is the foundation of good human health. Poland has an enviable reputation for 'real food' – and it's thanks to you! But it's hanging by a thread. The staples of the Polish diet, you have surely noticed, are being synthesised into something distinctly unpalatable. Suddenly 'soya', most likely genetically modified, has appeared as a significant component of nearly all commercial breads and many other bakery products (and, unfortunately, the diet of many farm animals). Sausages have lost their meaty quality and distinctive flavour, and most vegetables appear to have no flavour at all; chemical and colour infused margarines are replacing good farmhouse butters; genetically modified cooking oils are replacing real oils – and the first generation of semi-obese children are emerging out of the coca colarisation of the Polish diet.

If this looks like a mirror of 'Symptom USA' it is not surprising – many European countries (including my England) have copied the US model without having any idea of the huge price in human and environmental health that must be paid by going down this road to Armageddon.

Yet this is the diet that 'corporate agriculture' is *supposed* to be providing! It is the diet that government technocrats, pharmaceutical companies and genetic engineering exponents are serving to us because *we don't complain* about being treated like machines or rats in a laboratory experiment. And if we do complain, most do it in the living room or in bars – and not in the streets or in the centres of power where these decisions are made and where our voices cannot be ignored.

If we don't unite in our resistance – and now – we stand to lose one of the greatest natural treasures in Europe. Not only that, we will remain open to being ridiculed by our grandchildren for being accomplices in the destruction of our rural communities and for being open to being bought-out by the State. We farmers constitute an important line of resistance; there are still more of us than any other profession in the world. And we have something which many others do not have: independence and land. This also gives us a very real responsibility for the future. We have good reason to 'think ahead', much further than those only concerned with the next term of election.

In Poland, we have the numbers and the ability to stop the top down manipulation that is eroding the traditional, sustainable and proud rural heart beat. But at the same time we must continue to set an example as true trustees of the living earth. It is a real responsibility and **it means that we have to do more than just farm. It means we have to get up and get out to fight for the life to come.** It means not hiding away, but gathering our energies together and uniting to come face to face with the task at hand: To achieve proper terms, prices and secure conditions for the future of national, regional and local food production. Then standing firm against any further cynical political and corporate manipulation of time honoured, enduring food and farming traditions. Good food and time honoured sustainable farming practices are essential to the survival of human kind. We must lead the way in defeating the oppressive and destructive forces which currently appear to have forgotten this fact, or are trying to ignore it.

Julian Rose
January 2009